THE
# RICHEST
# MAN
IN
# BABYLON
IN **ACTION**

# THE
# RICHEST
# MAN
## IN
# BABYLON
## IN ACTION

## Based on the Classic Work
## by George S. Clason

NIGHTINGALE-CONANT LEARNING SYSTEM

MEDIA

# Contents

# Preface

George Samuel Clason's book *The Richest Man in Babylon* is one of the great inspirational classics of the twentieth century. It was originally published in 1926, before the Great Depression. The book began as a series of informational pamphlets. Banks and insurance companies began to distribute them, and the most famous ones were eventually compiled into a book. More than 2 million copies have been sold. In *The Richest Man in Babylon in Action*, you'll learn how to take the classic ideas from *The Richest Man in Babylon* and update them.

You probably know that wealth magnifies power and happiness, but do you know the Seven Cures for a Lean Purse? Is there such a thing as a Goddess of Good Luck? What are the Five Laws of Gold, and how can you use them to make you rich? These are just some of the questions we'll be answering.

This book contains the complete original text of The *Rich Man of Babylon*, including the original foreword, with some minor corrections and modernization of the spelling. At that end of each chapter, I'll recap the important parts of the story and discover some practical tips on how you can apply these lessons to your own twenty-first-century life. You may not want to invest your gold in a camel (you'll learn more about that as our story begins), but we'll talk about modern techniques for making your money work for you. We have tips and ideas from experts in wealth building, debt reduction, and real-estate investing as well as other stories and ideas from modern life.

Before we get started, let me make some suggestions as to how to get the most out of this book. We'll go through the original text. Then, after each chapter, we'll apply the ideas to your life. It would be a good idea to get a notebook or a journal so that you can do the exercises.

At the end of each session is a brief segment called the Babylon Builder. This is a concise recap of the core ideas and action steps that you can take to build your own personal empire. By the end, you'll have everything you need to become the richest man or woman in Babylon, or whatever city you're in.

*—Dan Strutzel*

# Foreword

Our prosperity as a nation depends upon the personal financial prosperity of each of us as individuals.

This book deals with the personal successes of each of us. Success means accomplishments as the result of our own efforts and abilities. Proper preparation is the key to our success. Our acts can be no wiser than our thoughts. Our thinking can be no wiser than our understanding.

This book of cures for lean purses has been termed a guide to financial understanding. That, indeed, is its purpose: to offer those who are ambitious for financial success an insight which will aid them to acquire money, to keep money, and to make their surpluses earn more money.

In the pages which follow, we are taken back to Babylon, the cradle in which was nurtured the basic principles of finance now recognized and used the world over.

To new readers, the author is happy to extend the wish that its pages may contain for them the same inspiration for growing bank accounts, greater financial successes and the solution of difficult personal financial problems so enthusiastically reported by readers from coast to coast.

To the business executives who have distributed these tales in such generous quantities to friends, relatives, employees and associates, the author takes this opportunity to express his gratitude. No endorsement could be higher than that of practical men who appreciate its teachings because they themselves have worked up to important successes by applying the very principles it advocates.

Babylon became the wealthiest city of the ancient world because its citizens were the richest people of their time. They appreciated the value of money. They practiced sound financial principles in acquiring money, keeping money and making their money earn more money. They provided for themselves what we all desire —incomes for the future.

*—George S. Clason*

# ONE
# An Historical
# Sketch of Babylon

In the pages of history, there lives no city more glamorous than Babylon. Its very name conjures visions of wealth and splendor. Its treasures of gold and jewels were fabulous. One naturally pictures such a wealthy city as located in a suitable setting of tropical luxury surrounded by rich, natural resources of forests and mines. Such was not the case. It was located beside the Euphrates River in a flat, arid valley. It had no forests, no mines, not even stone for building. It was not even located upon a natural trade route. The rainfall was insufficient to raise crops.

Babylon is an outstanding example of man's ability to achieve great objectives using whatever means are at his disposal. All of the resources supporting this large city were man-developed. All of its riches were man-made.

Babylon possessed just two natural resources—a fertile soil and water in the river. With one of the greatest engineering accomplishments of this or any other day, Babylonian engineers diverted the waters from the river by means of dams and immense irrigation canals. Far out across that arid valley went these canals to pour the life-giving waters over the fertile soil. This ranks among the first engineering feats known to history. Such abundant crops as were the reward of this irrigation system, the world had never seen before.

Fortunately, during its long existence, Babylon was ruled by successive lines of kings to which conquests and plunder were but incidental. While it engaged in many wars, most of these were local or defensive against ambitious conquerors from other countries who coveted the fabulous treasures of Babylon. The outstanding rulers of Babylon live in history because of their wisdom, enterprise, and justice. Babylon produced no strutting monarchs who sought to conquer the known world that all nations might pay homage to their egotism.

As a city, Babylon exists no more. When those energizing human forces that built and maintained the city for thousands of years were withdrawn, it soon became a deserted ruin. The site of the city is in Asia about 600 miles east of the Suez Canal, just north of the Persian Gulf. The latitude is about thirty degrees above the equator, practically the same as that of Yuma, Arizona. It possessed a climate similar to that of this American city—hot and dry.

Today this valley of the Euphrates, once a populous, irrigated farming district, is again a windswept, arid waste. Scant grass and desert shrubs strive for existence against the wind-blown sands. Gone are the fertile fields, the mammoth cities, and the long caravans of rich merchandise. Nomadic vans of Arabs securing a scant living by tending small herds are the only inhabitants. Such it has been since about the beginning of the Christian era.

Dotting this valley are earthen hills. For centuries, they were considered by travelers to be nothing else. The attention of archaeologists were finally attracted to them because of broken pieces of pottery and brick washed down by the occasional rainstorms. Expeditions financed by European and American museums were sent here to excavate and see what could be found. Picks and shovels soon proved these hills to be ancient cities—city graves, they might well be called.

Babylon was one of these. Over it, for something like twenty centuries, the winds had scattered the desert dust. Built originally of brick, all exposed walls had disintegrated and gone back to earth once more. Such is Babylon, the wealthy city today. A heap of dirt so long abandoned that no living person even knew its name until it was discovered by carefully removing the refuse of centuries from the streets and the fallen wreckage of its noble temples and palaces.

Many scientists consider the civilization of Babylon and other cities in this valley to be the oldest of which there is a definite record. Positive dates have been proved reaching back 8000 years. An interesting fact in this connection is the means used to determine these dates. Uncovered in the ruins of Babylon were descriptions of an eclipse of the sun. Modern astronomers readily computed the time when such an eclipse, visible in Babylon, occurred and thus established a known relationship between their calendar and our own.

In this way, we have proved that 8,000 years ago, the Sumerites, who inhabited Babylonia, were living in walled cities. One can only conjecture for how many centuries previous such cities had existed. Their inhabitants were not mere barbarians living within protecting walls. They were an educated and enlightened people. So far as written history goes, they were the first engineers, the first astronomers, the first mathematicians, the first financiers, and the first people to have a written language.

Mention has already been made of the irrigation systems, which transformed the arid valley into an agricultural paradise. The remains of these canals can still be traced, although they are mostly filled with accumulated sand. Some of them were of such size that, when empty of water, a dozen horses could be ridden abreast along their bottoms. In size, they compare favorably with the largest canals in Colorado and Utah.

In addition to irrigating the valley lands, Babylonian engineers completed another project of similar magnitude. By means of an elaborate drainage system, they reclaimed an immense area of swampland at the mouths of the Euphrates and Tigris Rivers and put this under cultivation.

Herodotus, the Greek traveler and historian, visited Babylon while it was in its prime and has given us the only known description by an outsider. His writings give a graphic description of the city and some of the unusual customs of its people. He mentions the remarkable fertility of the soil and the bountiful harvest of wheat and barley, which they produced.

The glory of Babylon has faded, but its wisdom has been preserved for us. For this we are indebted to their form of records. In that distant day, the use of paper had not been invented. Instead, they laboriously engraved their writings upon tablets of moist clay. When completed, these were baked and became hard tile. In size, they were about six by eight inches, and an inch in thickness.

These clay tablets, as they are commonly called, were used much as we use modern forms of writing. Upon them were engraved legends, poetry, history, transcriptions of royal decrees, the laws of the land, titles to property, promissory notes, and even letters which were dispatched by messengers to distant cities.

From these clay tablets, we are permitted an insight into the intimate personal affairs of the people. For example, one tablet, evidently from the records of a country storekeeper, relates that upon the given date a certain named customer brought in a cow and exchanged it for seven sacks of wheat, three being delivered at the time, and the other four to await the customer's pleasure.

Safely buried in the wrecked cities, archeologists have recovered entire libraries of these tablets, hundreds of thousands of them.

One of the outstanding wonders of Babylon was the immense wall surrounding the city. The ancients ranked them with the Great Pyramid of Egypt as belonging to the Seven Wonders of the World. Queen Semiramis is credited with having erected the first walls during the early history of the city. Modern excavators have been unable to find any trace of the original walls. Nor is their exact height known. From mention made by early writers, it is estimated that they were about fifty to sixty feet high, faced on the outer side with burnt brick and further protected by a deep moat of water.

The later and more famous walls were started about 600 years before the time of Christ by King Nabopolassar. He planned the rebuilding on such a scale that he did not live to see the work finished. This was left to his son, Nebuchadnezzar, whose name is familiar in biblical history.

The height and length of these later walls staggers belief. They are reported upon reliable authority to have been about 160 feet high, the equivalent of the height of a modern fifteen-story office building. The total length is estimated as between nine and eleven miles. So wide was the top that a six-horse chariot could be driven around them. Of this tremendous structure, little now remains except portions of the foundations and the moat. In addition to the ravages of the elements, the Arabs completed the destruction by quarrying the brick for building purposes elsewhere.

Against the walls of Babylon marched, in turn, the victorious armies of almost every conqueror of that age of wars of conquest. A host of kings laid siege to Babylon but always in vain. Invading armies of that day were not to be considered lightly. Historians speak of such units as 10,000 horsemen, 25,000 chariots, 1,200 regiments of foot soldiers with 1,000 men to the regiment. Often two or three years of preparation would be required to assemble war materials and depots of food along the proposed line of march.

The city of Babylon was organized much like a modern city. There were streets and shops. Peddlers offered their wares through residential districts. Priests officiated in magnificent temples. Within the city was an inner enclosure for the royal palaces. The walls about this were said to have been higher than those about the city.

The Babylonians were skilled in the arts. These included sculpture, painting, weaving, gold working, and the manufacture of metal weapons and agricultural implements. Their jewelers created most artistic jewelry. Many samples have been recovered from the graves of its wealthy citizens and are now on exhibition in the leading museums of the world.

At a very early period, when the rest of the world was still hacking at trees with stone-headed axes, or hunting and fighting with flint-pointed spears and arrows, the Babylonians were using axes, spears, and arrows with metal heads.

The Babylonians were clever financiers and traders. So far as we know, they were the original inventors of money as a means of exchange, of promissory notes, and written titles to property.

Babylon was never entered by hostile armies until about 540 years before the birth of Christ. Even then, the walls were not captured. The story of the fall of Babylon is most unusual. Cyrus, one of the great conquerors of that period, intended to attack the city and hoped to take its impregnable walls. Advisors of Nabonidus, the king of Babylon, persuaded him to go forth to meet Cyrus and give him battle without waiting for the city to be besieged.

In the succeeding defeat of the Babylonian army, it fled away from the city. Cyrus thereupon entered the open gates and took the possession without resistance.

Thereafter the power and prestige of that city gradually waned until, in the course of a few hundred years, it was eventually abandoned, deserted, left for the winds and storms to level once again to that desert earth from which its grandeur had originally been built. Babylon had fallen, never to rise again, but to it, civilization owes much.

The eons of time have crumbed to dust the proud walls of its temples, but the wisdom of Babylon endures.

Money is the medium by which earthly success is measured.

Money makes possible the enjoyment of the best the earth affords.

Money is plentiful for those who understand the simple laws which govern its acquisition.

Money is governed today by the same laws which controlled it when prosperous men thronged the streets of Babylon 6,000 years ago.

# TWO
# The Man Who Desired Gold

Bansir, the chariot builder of Babylon, was thoroughly discouraged. From his seat upon the low wall surrounding his property, he gazed sadly at his simple home and the open workshop, in which stood a partially completed chariot.

His wife frequently appeared at the open door. Her furtive glances in his direction reminded him that the meal bag was almost empty and he should be at work finishing the chariot, hammering and hewing, polishing and painting, stretching taut the leather over the wheel rims, preparing it for delivery so he could collect from his wealthy customer.

Nevertheless, his fat, muscular body sat stolidly upon the wall. His slow mind was struggling patiently with a problem for which he could find no answer. The hot, tropical sun, so typical of this valley of the Euphrates, beat down upon him mercilessly. Beads of perspiration formed upon his brow and trickled down unnoticed to lose themselves in the hairy jungle on his chest.

Beyond his home towered the high terraced wall surrounding the king's palace. Nearby, cleaving the blue heavens, was the painted tower of the Temple of Bel. In the shadow of such grandeur was his simple home and many others far less neat and well cared for. Babylon was like this—a mixture of grandeur and squalor, of dazzling wealth and direst poverty, crowded together without plan or system within the protecting walls of the city.

Behind him, had he cared to turn and look, the noisy chariots of the rich jostled and crowded aside the sandaled tradesmen as well as the barefooted beggars. Even the rich were forced to turn into the gutters to clear the way for the long lines of slave water carriers, on the king's business, each bearing a heavy goatskin of water to be poured upon the Hanging Gardens.

Bansir was too engrossed in his own problem to hear or heed the confused hubbub of the busy city. It was the unexpected twanging of the strings from a familiar lyre that aroused him from his reverie. He turned and looked into the sensitive, smiling face of his best friend—Kobbi the musician.

"May the gods bless thee with great liberality, my good friend," began Kobbi with an elaborate salute. "Yet, it doth appear they have already been so generous thou needest not to labor. I rejoice with thee in thy good fortune. More, I would even share it with thee. Pray, from thy purse, which must be bulging, else thou wouldst be busy in your shop, extract but two humble shekels and lend them to me until after the noblemen's feast this night. Thou wilt not miss them ere they are returned."

"If I did have two shekels," Bansir responded gloomily, "to no one could I lend them, not even to you, my best of friends, for they would be my fortune, my entire fortune. No one lends his entire fortune, not even to his best friend."

"What?" exclaimed Kobbi with genuine surprise. "Thou hast not one shekel in thy purse, yet sit like a statue upon a wall? Why not complete that chariot? How else canst thou provide for thy noble appetite? 'Tis not like thee, my friend. Where is thy endless energy? Doth something distress thee? Have the gods brought to thee troubles?"

"A torment from the gods it must be," Bansir agreed. "It began with a dream, a senseless dream, in which I thought I was a man of means. From my belt hung a handsome purse, heavy with coins. There were shekels which I cast with careless freedom to the beggars. There were pieces of silver with which I did buy finery for my wife and whatever I did desire for myself. There were pieces of gold, which made me feel assured of the future and unafraid to spend the silver. A glorious feeling of contentment was within me. You would not have known me for thy hardworking friend, nor wouldst have known my wife, so free from wrinkles was her face and shining with happiness. She was again the smiling maiden of our early married days."

"A pleasant dream, indeed," commented Kobbi, "but why should such pleasant feelings as it aroused turn thee into a glum statue upon the wall?"

"Why, indeed! Because when I awoke and remembered how empty was my purse, a feeling of rebellion swept over me. Let us talk it over together, for as the sailors do say, we ride in the same boat, we two. As youngsters, we went together to the priests to learn wisdom. As young men, we shared each other's pleasures. As grown men, we have always been close friends. We have been contented subjects of our kind. We have been satisfied to work long hours and spend our earnings freely. We have earned much coin in the years that have passed, yet to know the joys that come from wealth, we must dream about them. Bah! Are we more than dumb sheep? We live in the richest city in all the world. The travelers do say none equals it in wealth. About us is much display of wealth, but of it we ourselves have naught. After half a lifetime of hard labor, thou my best of friends, hast an empty purse and sayest to me, 'May I borrow such a trifle as two shekels until after the noblemen's feast this night?' Then what do I reply? Do I say, 'Here is my purse; its contents will I gladly share'? No, I admit that my purse is as empty as thine. What is the matter? Why cannot we acquire silver and gold more than enough for food and robes?

"Consider also our sons," Bansir continued. "Are they not following in the footsteps of their fathers? Need they and their families and their sons and their sons' families live all their lives in the midst of such treasurers of gold, and yet, like us, be content to banquet upon sour goat's milk and porridge?"

"Never, in all the years of our friendship, didst thou talk like this before, Bansir." Kobbi was puzzled.

"Never in all those years did I think like this before. From early dawn until darkness stopped me, I have labored to build the finest chariots any man could make, soft-heartedly hoping some day the gods would recognize my worthy deeds and bestow upon me great prosperity. This they have never done. At last, I realize this they will never do. Therefore my heart is sad. I wish to be a man of means. I wish to own lands and cattle, to have fine robes and coins in my purse. I am willing to work for these things with all the strength in my back, with all the skill in my hands, with all the cunning in my mind, but I wish my labors to be fairly rewarded. What is the matter with us? Again I ask you, why cannot we have our just share of the good things so plentiful for those who have the gold with which to buy them?"

"Would I knew an answer!" Kobbi replied. "No better than thou am I satisfied. My earnings from my lyre are quickly gone. Often must I plan and scheme that my family be not hungry. Also, within my breast is a deep longing for a lyre large enough that it may truly sing the strains of music that do surge through my mind. With such an instrument could I make music finer than even the king has heard before."

"Such a lyre thou shouldst have. No man in all Babylon could make it sing more sweetly, could make it sing so sweetly, not only the king but the gods themselves would be delighted. But how mayest thou secure it while we both of us are as poor as the king's slaves? Listen to the bell. Here they come." He pointed to the long column of half-naked, sweating water bearers plodding laboriously up the narrow street from the river. Five abreast they marched, each bent under a heavy goatskin of water.

"A fine figure of a man, he who doth lead them." Kobbi indicated the wearer of the bell who marched in front without a load. "A prominent man in his own country, 'tis easy to see."

"There are many good figures in the line," Bansir agreed, "as good men as we. Tall, blond men from the north, laughing black men from the south, little brown men from the nearer countries, all marching together from the river to the gardens, back and forth, day after day, year after year. Naught of happiness to look forward to. Beds of straw upon which to sleep—hard grain porridge to eat. Pity the poor brutes, Kobbi!"

"Pity them I do. Yet thou dost make me see how little better off are we, free men though we call ourselves."

"That is truth, Kobbi, unpleasant thought though it be. We do not wish to go on year after year living slavish lives, working, working, working, getting nowhere!"

"Might we not find out how others acquire gold and do as they do?" Kobbi inquired.

"Perhaps there is some secret we might learn if we but sought from those who knew," replied Bansir thoughtfully.

"This very day," suggested Kobbi, "I did pass our old friend, Arkad, riding in his golden chariot. This I will say: He did not look over my humble head as many in his station might consider his right. Instead, he did wave his hand that all onlookers might see him pay greetings and bestow his smile of friendship upon Kobbi, the musician."

"He is claimed to be the richest man in all Babylon," Bansir mused.

"So rich the king is said to seek his gold in aid in affairs of the treasury," Kobbi replied.

"So rich," Bansir interrupted, "I fear if I should meet him in the darkness of the night, I should lay my hands upon his fat wallet."

"Nonsense," reproved Kobbi, "a man's wealth is not in the purse he carries. A fat purse quickly empties if there be no golden stream to refill it. Arkad has an income that constantly keeps his purse full, no matter how liberally he spends."

"Income, that is the thing," ejaculated Bansir. "I wish an income that will keep flowing into my purse whether I sit upon the wall or travel to far lands. Arkad must know how a man can make an income for himself. Dost suppose it is something he could make clear to a mind as slow as mine?"

"Methinks he did teach his knowledge to his son, Nomasir," Kobbi responded. "Did he not go to Nineveh and, so it is told at the inn, become, without aid from his father, one of the richest men in that city?"

"Kobbi, thou bringest to me a rare thought." A new light gleamed in Bansir's eyes. "It costs nothing to ask wise advice from a good friend, and Arkad was always that. Never mind though our purses be as empty as the falcon's nest of a year ago. Let that not detain us. We are weary of being without gold in the midst of plenty. We wish to become men of means. Come, let us go to Arkad, and ask how we also may acquire incomes for ourselves."

"Thou speakest with true inspiration, Bansir. Thou bringeth to my mind a new understanding. Thou makest me to realize the reason why we have never found any measure of wealth. We have never sought it. Thou hast labored patiently to build the staunchest chariots in Babylon. To that purpose was devoted your best endeavors. Therefore at it thou didst succeed. I strove to become a skillful lyre player. And at it I did succeed.

"In those things toward which we exerted our best endeavors we succeeded. The gods were content to let us continue thus. Now, at last, we see a light, bright like that from the rising sun. It biddeth us to learn more that we may prosper more. With a new understanding we shall find honorable ways to accomplish our desires."

"Let us go to Arkad this very day," Bansir urged. "Also, let us ask other friends of our boyhood days, who have fared no better than ourselves, to join us that they, too, may share in his wisdom."

"Thou wert ever thus thoughtful of thy friends, Bansir. Therefore hast thou many friends. It shall be as thou sayest. We go this day and take them with us."

---

# ❧ Dan ❧

Like many modern cities, Babylon was a land of great disparity between the rich and the poor. In the story we just heard, Bansir was a simple Babylonian chariot builder. As he sat and looked over his small home and the unfinished chariot in his workshop, he wondered why he worked so hard and yet remained so poor.

Kobbi, who was Bansir's friend and a musician, came up and greeted him happily. He wanted to borrow some money until the feast later that night. Unfortunately, Bansir didn't have it. A lot of us can relate to this. To the outside world, it looks like we have plenty, but in reality, we don't even have two shekels to lend to our friend.

Bansir told Kobbi that he dreamed of possessing fabulous wealth, but that he was sitting around moping because his reality didn't match up to his dreams. Again, this is something most of us can relate to. We have all these goals and dreams, but when we look at our life and our unfinished plans, we get disappointed.

The two friends reflected on how much money they had earned over the course of their lives and had little they had to show for it now. Can you relate?

Many people work for twenty, thirty, or forty years and don't have enough money to retire. In fact, according to a recent article in *The New York Times,* nearly four in ten workers over age sixty-two say they have delayed their retirement because of the recession that began at the end of 2007. Last year, in the United States, almost a third of people ages sixty-five to sixty-nine were still in the labor force.

Bansir was starting to think that future generations of his family would have to toil and struggle as well. Kobbi, the optimist, wondered if it was possible to become wealthy by learning what the wealthy do and mimicking it. As you heard in the story, Bansir agreed and decided that there must be a secret to acquiring gold. Bansir and Kobbi decided to ask their old friend, Arkad, who was the richest man in Babylon, to teach them the secrets to becoming wealthy.

Can you relate to this? Did you once have goals and dreams, but have nothing to show for your hard work? What are some of the goals and dreams you had?

It's time for your first exercise. Reflect on the lifestyle you wanted a long time ago. How much money did you think you would have by now? Did you think you would have certain material possessions? Did you plan to have achieved certain career goals?

Of course, like Bansir and Kobbi as they observed the slaves, you're not as badly off as some people, but how does your reality fit with those dreams you had long ago? Write your answers down in your journal.

Before you move on to the next chapter, take some time to dream big. If you could become the richest man or woman in Babylon, what would that look like? Write some of those big thoughts in your journal.

### Babylon Builder

The key idea in this chapter is that even if you're sitting around depressed because you don't have financial wealth, it's not too late. You can dream big things, and by learning to do what the wealthy do, you can become wealthy too.

For action steps, you started a journal, and in it you wrote down some of the dreams you used to have, and then you compared that list with the reality of how you're living now. You also spent some time dreaming big. Let's move onto the next chapter now, where Bansir meets with his rich friend, Arkad.

# THREE

# The Richest Man in Babylon

In old Babylon there once lived a certain very rich man named Arkad. Far and wide he was famed for his great wealth. Also was he famed for his liberality. He was generous in his charities. He was generous with his family. He was liberal in his own expenses, but nevertheless each year his wealth increased more rapidly than he spent it.

And there were certain friends of younger days who came to him and said, "You, Arkad, are more fortunate than we. You have become the richest man in all Babylon while we struggle for existence. You can wear the finest garments and you can enjoy the rarest foods, while we must be content if we can clothe our families in raiment that is presentable and feed them as best we can.

"Yet once we were equal. We studied under the same master. We played in the same games. And in neither the studies nor the games did you outshine us, and in the years since, you have been no more an honorable citizen than we. Nor have you worked harder or more faithfully, insofar as we can judge. Why, then, should a fickle fate single you out to enjoy all the good things of life and ignore us, who are equally deserving?"

Thereupon Arkad remonstrated with them, saying, "If you have not acquired more than a bare existence in the years since we were youths, it is because you either have failed to learn the laws that govern the building of wealth, or else you do not observe them.

"Fickle Fate is a vicious goddess who brings no permanent good to anyone. On the contrary, she brings ruin to almost every man upon whom she showers unearned gold. She makes wanton spenders, who soon dissipate all they receive and are left beset by overwhelming appetites and desires they have not the ability to gratify. Yet others, whom she favors, become misers and hoard their wealth, fearing to spend what they have, knowing they do not possess the ability to replace it. They further are beset by fear of robbers and doom themselves to lives of emptiness and secret misery.

"Others there probably are, who can take unearned gold and add to it and continue to be happy and contented citizens. But so few are they, I know of them but by hearsay. Think you of the men who have inherited sudden wealth, and see if these things are not so."

His friends admitted that of the men they knew who had inherited wealth these words were true, and they besought him to explain to them how he had become possessed of so much prosperity, so he continued: "In my youth I looked about me and saw all the good things there were to bring happiness and contentment, and I realized that wealth increased the potency of all these. Wealth is a power. With wealth many things are possible.

"One may ornament the home with the richest of furnishings. One may sail the distant seas. One may feast on the delicacies of far lands.

"One may buy the ornaments of the gold worker and the stone polisher.

"One may even build mighty temples for the gods.

"One may do all these things and many others in which there is delight for the senses and gratification for the soul.

"And when I realized all this, I decided to myself that I would claim my share of the good things of life. I would not be one of those who stand afar off, enviously watching others enjoy. I would not be content to clothe myself in the cheapest raiment that looked respectable. I would not be satisfied with the lot of a poor man. On the contrary, I would make myself a guest at this banquet of good things.

"Being, as you know, the son of a humble merchant, one of a large family with no hope of an inheritance, and not being endowed, as you have so frankly said, with superior powers or wisdom, I decided that if I was to achieve what I desired, time and study would be required.

"As for time, all men have it in abundance. You, each of you, have let slip by sufficient time to have made yourselves wealthy. Yet, you admit you have nothing to show except your good families, of which you can be justly proud.

"As for study, did not our wise teacher teach us that learning was of two kinds, the one kind being the things we learned and knew, and the other being the training that taught us how to find out what we did not know?

"Therefore did I decide to find out how one might accumulate wealth, and when I had found out, to make this my task and do it well. For is it not wise that we should enjoy while we dwell in the brightness of the sunshine, for sorrows enough shall descend upon us when we depart for the darkness of the world of spirit?

"I found employment as a scribe in the hall of records, and long hours each day I labored upon the clay tablets. Week after week and month after month, I labored, yet for my earnings I had naught to show. Food and clothing and penance to the gods, and other things of which I could remember not what, absorbed all my earnings, but my determination did not leave me.

"And one day Algamish the moneylender came to the house of the city master and ordered a copy of the Ninth Law, and he said to me, 'I must have this in two days, and if the task is done by that time, two coppers will I give to thee.'

"So I labored hard, but the law was long, and when Algamish returned, the task was unfinished. He was angry, and had I been his slave, he would have beaten me, but knowing the city master would not permit him to injure me, I was unafraid, so I said to him, 'Algamish, you are a very rich man. Tell me how I may also become rich, and all night I will carve upon the clay, and when the sun rises it shall be completed.'

"He smiled at me and replied, 'You are a forward knave, but we will call it a bargain.'

"All that night I carved, though my back pained and the smell of the wick made my head ache until my eyes could hardly see, but when he returned at sunup, the tablets were complete.

"'Now,' I said, 'tell me what you promised.'

"'You have fulfilled your part of our bargain, my son,' he said to me kindly, 'and I am ready to fulfill mine. I will tell you these things you wish to know because I am becoming an old man, and an old tongue loves to wag. And when youth comes to age for advice, he receives the wisdom of years. But too often does youth think that age knows only the wisdom of days that are gone, and therefore profits not. But remember this: the sun that shines today is the sun that shone when thy father was born, and will still be shining when thy last grandchild shall pass into the darkness. "'The thoughts of youth,' he continued, 'are bright lights that shine forth like the meteors that oft make brilliant the sky, but the wisdom of age is like the fixed stars that shine so unchanged that the sailor may depend upon them to steer his course.

"'Mark you well my words, for if you do not you will fail to grasp the truth that I will tell you, and you will think that your night's work has been in vain.'

"Then he looked at me shrewdly from under his shaggy brows and said in a low, forceful tone, 'I found the road to wealth when I decided that a part of all I earned was mine to keep. And so will you.'"

"Then he continued to look at me with a glance that I could feel pierce me, but said no more.

"'Is that all?' I asked.

"'That was sufficient to change the heart of a sheep-herder into the heart of a moneylender,' he replied.

"'But all I earn is mine to keep, is it not?' I demanded.

"'Far from it,' he replied. 'Do you not pay the garment maker? Do you not pay the sandalmaker? Do you not pay for the things you eat? Can you live in Babylon without spending? What have you to show for your earnings of the past month? What for the past year? Fool, you pay to everyone but yourself. Dullard, you labor for others. As well be a slave and work for what your master gives you to eat and wear. If you did keep for yourself one-tenth of all you earn, how much would you have in ten years?'

"My knowledge of the numbers did not forsake me, and I answered, 'As much as I earn in one year.'

"'You speak but half the truth,' he retorted. 'Every gold piece you save is a slave to work for you. Every copper it earns is its child that also can earn for you. If you would become wealthy, then what you save must earn, and its children must earn, that all may help to give to you the abundance you crave.

"'You think I cheat you for your long night's work,' he continued, 'but I am paying you a thousand times over if you have the intelligence to grasp the truth I offer you.

"'A part of all you earn is yours to keep. It should not be less than a tenth, no matter how little you earn. It can be as much more as you can afford. Pay yourself first. Do not buy from the clothesmaker and the sandalmaker more than you can pay out of the rest and still have enough for food and charity and penance to the gods.

"'Wealth, like a tree, grows from a tiny seed. The first copper you save is the seed from which your tree of wealth shall grow. The sooner you plant that seed, the sooner shall the tree grow, and the more faithfully you nourish and water that tree with consistent savings, the sooner may you bask in contentment beneath its shade.'

"So saying, he took his tablets and went away.

"I thought much about what he had said to me, and it seemed reasonable. So I decided that I would try it. Each time I was paid, I took one from each ten pieces of copper and hid it away, and strange as it may seem, I was no shorter of funds than before. I noticed little difference, as I managed to get along without it. But often I was tempted, as my hoard began to grow, to spend it for some of the good things the merchants displayed, brought by camels and ships from the land of the Phoenicians. But I wisely refrained.

"A twelfth month after Algamish had gone, he again returned and said to me, 'Son, have you paid to yourself not less than one tenth of all you have earned for the past year?'

"I answered proudly, 'Yes, master, I have.'"

"'That is good,' he answered, beaming upon me, 'and what have you done with it?'

"'I have given it to Azmur, the brickmaker, who told me he was traveling over the far seas and in Tyre he would buy for me the rare jewels of the Phoenicians. When he returns, we shall sell these at high prices and divide the earnings.'

"'Every fool must learn,' he growled, 'but why trust the knowledge of a brickmaker about jewels? Would you go to the breadmaker to inquire about the stars? No. By my tunic, you would go to the astrologer, if you had power to think. Your savings are gone, youth, you have jerked your wealth tree up by the roots. But plant another. Try again, and next time if you would have advice about jewels, go to the jewel merchant. If you would know the truth about sheep, go to the herdsman. Advice is one thing that is freely given away, but watch that you take only what is worth having. He who takes advice about his savings from one who is inexperienced in such matters shall pay with his savings for proving the falsity of their opinions.' Saying this, he went away.

"And it was as he said. For the Phoenicians are scoundrels and sold to Azmur worthless bits of glass that looked like gems. But as Algamish had bid me, I again saved each tenth copper, for I now had formed the habit, and it was no longer difficult. Again, twelve months later, Algamish came to the room of the scribes and addressed me. 'What progress have you made since last I saw you?'

"'I have paid myself faithfully,' I replied, 'and my savings I have entrusted to Agger the shieldmaker to buy bronze, and each fourth month he does pay me the rental.'

"'That is good, and what do you do with the rental?'

"'I do have a great feast with honey and fine wine and spiced cake. Also, I have bought me a scarlet tunic, and someday I shall buy me a young ass upon which to ride.'

"To which Algamish laughed, 'You do eat the children of your savings. Then how do you expect them to work for you, and how can they have children that will also work for you? First, get thee an army of golden slaves, and then many a rich banquet may you enjoy without regret.' So saying, he again went away.

"Nor did I again see him for two years, when he once more returned and his face was full of deep lines and his eyes drooped, for he was becoming a very old man, and he said to me, 'Arkad, hast thou yet achieved the wealth thou dreamed of?'

"And I answered, 'Not yet all that I desire, but some I have and it earns more, and its earnings earn more.'

"'And, do you still take the advice of brickmakers?'

"'About brickmaking they give good advice,' I retorted.

"'Arkad,' he continued, 'you have learned your lessons well. You first learned to live upon less than you could earn. Next, you learned to seek advice from those who were competent through their own experiences to give it. And lastly, you have learned to make gold work for you.

"'You have taught yourself how to acquire money, how to keep it, and how to use it. Therefore you are competent for a responsible position. I am becoming an old man. My sons think only of spending and give no thought to earning. My interests are great and, I fear, too much for me to look after. If you will go to Nippur and look after my lands there, I shall make you my partner, and you shall share in my estate.'

"So I went to Nippur and took charge of his holdings, which were large. And because I was full of ambition and because I had mastered the three laws of successfully handling wealth, I was enabled to increase greatly the value of his properties.

"So I prospered much, and when the spirit of Algamish departed for the sphere of darkness, I did share in his estate as he had arranged under the law."

So spake Arkad, and when he had finished his tale, one of his friends said, "You were indeed fortunate that Algamish made of you an heir."

"Fortunate only in that I had the desire to prosper before I first met him. For four years did I not prove my definiteness of purpose by keeping one-tenth of all earned? Would you call a fisherman lucky who for years so studied the habits of the fish that with each changing wind he could cast his nets about them? Opportunity is a haughty goddess who wastes no time with those who are unprepared."

"You had strong willpower to keep on after you lost your first year's savings. You are unusual in that way," spoke up another.

"Willpower!" retorted Arkad. "What nonsense. Do you think willpower gives a man the strength to lift a burden the camel cannot carry, or to draw a load the oxen cannot budge? Willpower is but the unflinching purpose to carry a task you set for yourself to fulfillment. If I set for myself a task, be it ever so trifling, I shall see it through. How else shall I have confidence in myself to do important things? Should I say to myself, 'For a hundred days as I walk across the bridge into the city, I will pick from the road a pebble and cast it into the stream,' I would do it. If on the seventh day I passed by without remembering, I would not say to myself, 'Tomorrow I will cast two pebbles, which will do as well.' Instead I would retrace my steps and cast the pebble. Nor on the twentieth day would I say to myself, 'Arkad, this is useless. What does it avail you to cast a pebble every day? Throw in a handful and be done with it.' No, I would not say that, nor do it. When I set a task for myself, I complete it. Therefore I am careful not to start difficult and impractical tasks, because I love leisure.'"

And then another friend spoke up and said, "If what you tell is true, and it does seem, as you have said, reasonable, then being so simple, if all men did it, there would not be enough wealth to go around."

"Wealth grows wherever men exert energy," Arkad replied. "If a rich man builds him a new palace, is the gold he pays out gone? No. The brickmaker has part of it, and the laborer has part of it, and the artist has part of it, and everyone who labors upon the house has part of it. Yet when the palace is completed, is it not worth all it cost, and is the ground upon which it stands not worth more because it is there, and is the ground that adjoins it not worth more because it is there? Wealth grows in magic ways. No man can prophesy the limit of it. Have not the Phoenicians built great cities on barren coasts with the wealth that comes from their ships of commerce on the seas?"

"What then do you advise us to do that we also may become rich?" asked still another of his friends. "The years have passed, and we are no longer young men and we have nothing put by."

"I advise that you take the wisdom of Algamish and say to yourselves, 'A part of all I earn is mine to keep.' Say it in the morning when you first arise. Say it at noon. Say it at night. Say it each hour of every day. Say it to yourself until the words stand out like letters of fire across the sky. Impress yourself with the idea. Fill yourself with the thought.

"Then take whatever portion seems wise. Let it be not less than one tenth, and lay it by. Arrange your other expenditures to do this if necessary, but lay by that portion first. Soon you will realize what a rich feeling it is to own a treasure upon which you alone have claim. As it grows, it will stimulate you. A new joy of life will thrill you. Greater efforts will come to you to earn more, for of your increased earnings, will not the same percentage be also yours to keep?

"Then learn to make the treasure work for you. Make it your slave. Make its children and its children's children work for you.

"Insure an income for thy future. Look thou at the aged and forget not that in the days to come thou also will be numbered among them. Therefore invest thy treasure with greatest caution, that it be not lost. Usurious rates of return are deceitful sirens that sing but to lure the unwary upon the rocks of loss and remorse.

"Provide also that thy family may not want should the gods call thee to their realms. For such protection it is always possible to make provision with small payments at regular intervals. Therefore the provident man delays not in expectation of a large sum becoming available for such a wise purpose.

"Counsel with wise men. Seek the advice of men whose daily work is handling money. Let them save you from such an error as I myself made in entrusting my money to the judgment of Azmur the brickmaker. A small return and a safe one is far more desirable than risk.

"Enjoy life while you are here. Do not overstrain or try to save too much. If one-tenth of all you earn is as much as you can comfortably keep, be content to keep this portion. Live otherwise according to your income and let not yourself get niggardly and afraid to spend. Life is good and life is rich, with things worthwhile and things to enjoy."

His friends thanked him and went away. Some were silent, because they had no imagination and could not understand. Some were sarcastic, because they thought that one so rich should divide with old friends not so fortunate, but some had in their eyes a new light. They realized that Algamish had come back each time to the room of the scribes because he was watching a man work his way out of darkness into light. When that man had found the light, a place awaited him. No one could fill that place until he had for himself worked out his own understanding, until he was ready for opportunity.

These latter were the ones, who, in the following years, frequently revisited Arkad, who received them gladly. He counseled with them and gave them freely of his wisdom, as men of broad experience are always glad to do, and he assisted them in so investing their savings that it would bring in a good interest with safety and would neither be lost nor entangled in investments that paid no dividends.

The turning point in these men's lives came upon that day when they realized the truth that had come from Algamish to Arkad and from Arkad to them. A part of all you earn is yours to keep.

# ⋖ Dan ⋗

As you just heard, Arkad, the richest man in Babylon was very generous with his family and gave a lot to charity. Even though he gave away a lot of money, his wealth continued to grow. Bansir and his friends met with Arkad and asked him why fate should make one man so wealthy when they all were equally deserving.

Arkad had replied that if they weren't wealthy, it was because they had failed to learn the laws of wealth building, or else they had failed to adhere to them. It's as author Larry Winget says, "You're broke because you want to be." If you don't learn the laws of wealth building, spend too much, or have debt, you're going to be broke forever.

Or as Arkad in our story said it, "If fickle fate brings wealth, wanton spending will take it away. If you get wealthy by luck, you'll cling fearfully to your fortune because you know you can't replace it."

Surely you've heard about lottery winners who lose it all within a few years of winning. Why? Because they didn't learn the laws of wealth, or they spend too much. Even many of those who still have the money become depressed and reclusive because they're afraid of losing it. Arkad said that few men can use their money wisely and can live happily.

During his youth, Arkad noticed that wealth magnifies power and happiness. He decided to be rich in order to acquire that which he desired. To be rich, he would have to immerse himself in the study of wealth accumulation, and once the laws were discovered, he would adhere closely to them. Did you hear that? He decided to become wealthy, but he didn't stop with just thinking about becoming wealthy. He took the action to learn the laws of wealth, and he stuck to them.

It's as Anthony Robbins says: "A real decision is measured by the fact that you've taken a new action. If there's no action, you haven't truly decided."

Now it's time for another exercise. In your journal, write down your commitment to immerse yourself in the study of wealth. Write it clearly, and in the present tense. It might sound something like this. "I, Dan Strutzel, have decided to become wealthy and am committed to studying the laws of wealth and then sticking to them."

Then write down five actions you'll take to immerse yourself in the study of wealth. One of them, of course, is reading this book, but what else? Maybe you'll subscribe to *The Wall Street Journal* or take a class on investing. Write down your commitment and your five actions in your journal.

Arkad also stated that it's not just what you know that's important, but also being able to learn what you don't already know. We all know people like that. By the time they graduate from high school or college, they've already learned everything they're going to learn. The end of school coincides with the end of learning, but that doesn't have to be you.

The iTunes store has hundreds of wealth-building podcasts, classes, and other audios in MP3 format. There are also Internet radio stations, such as blogtalkradio.com, where you can listen to talk shows with some of the most noted experts in wealth building. You don't need a special player or software, just a computer and an Internet connection.

One way to apply these ideas is to use modern technology to be constantly learning new wealth-building ideas. That's a lot better than just sitting around in Babylon. Just as you're learning the secrets of wealth from those who have achieved it, Arkad did the same thing.

He learned the secrets to wealth from a customer named Algamish. Algamish said that he became wealthy when he decided to keep a part of all he earned for himself, and he advised Arkad to do the same.

Algamish explained that if Arkad spent all his earnings, it meant that he labored for the merchants and not for himself. If he kept one-tenth of his earnings and didn't spend it, no matter what, then it would grow. When these savings accumulated, it would be the time for him to invest it, to make his wealth work for him.

We'll talk a bit more specifically in a later chapter about how to keep a part of what you earn for yourself. It took Arkad a couple of years to master the laws of wealth building. He made some mistakes. He gave his money to a brickmaker to invest in jewels. He lost all of his money. He then spent all of the interest that he'd earned instead of reinvesting it. Then, finally, he got it, and started to build real wealth.

When Algamish came back, he praised Arkad for having learned his lessons well. Here are the lessons. Number one, *live on less than you earn.* Number two, *seek advice from those who are competent from their own experience to give it.* Number three, *make your gold work for you.*

What does this mean for us? First of all, it means that no matter how many mistakes you've made in the past with money, you can overcome them. Many millionaires have lost their fortunes more than once but regained it. Donald Trump is probably the most famous example of this. His businesses have declared bankruptcy three times, and yet each time he bounced back.

Martha Stewart is another one. She made a critical mistake and went to prison. She was ousted as the CEO of the company that had her own name on it, but she too bounced back. No matter what mistakes you've made, it's not too late to bounce back.

Another thing we've learned is that it takes a lot of discipline to stick to your plan but that it's worth it. Finally, we learned that it's important to make our money work for us. We'll talk more about how to do this in a later chapter.

Arkad said that willpower is only an unflinching purpose to carry a task to completion. He said that if you set a task, you must complete it no matter what happens. So don't begin tasks lightly. He advised his friends to take the wisdom of Algamish and to prosper like him.

Remember: part of all I earn is mine to keep. Make gold your slave. Seek wise counsel, but don't stress out in practicing the principles. Instead, enjoy life while ensuring your future.

## Babylon Builder

The key ideas from this chapter are that even if you made a lot of mistakes about money, it's not too late. You can still become wealthy. You'll just have to decide to learn what you need to learn in order to become wealthy.

You have to follow the three lessons: live on less than you earn, seek the advice of those who are successful, and make your gold work for you. For action steps, you made a solid commitment to learning what you need to know to become wealthy. You identified some actions that you can take so that you can learn. If you haven't done these things yet, be sure you do before you go on to the next chapter, where we will learn the Seven Cures for a Lean Purse.

# FOUR
# Seven Cures
# for a Lean Purse

The glory of Babylon endures. Down through the ages its reputation comes to us as the richest of cities, its treasures as fabulous.

Yet it was not always so. The riches of Babylon were the results of the wisdom of its people. They first had to learn how to become wealthy.

When the good King Sargon returned to Babylon after defeating his enemies the Elamites, he was confronted with a serious situation. The royal chancellor explained it to the king thus, "After many years of great prosperity brought to our people because Your Majesty built the great irrigation canals and the mighty temples of the gods, now that these works are completed, the people seem unable to support themselves.

"The laborers are without employment. The merchants have few customers. The farmers are unable to sell their produce. The people have not enough gold to buy food."

"But where has all the gold gone that we spent for these great improvements?" demanded the king.

"It has found its way, I fear," responded the chancellor, "into the possession of a few very rich men of our city. It filtered through the fingers of most our people as quickly as the goat's milk goes through the strainer. Now that the stream of gold has ceased to flow, most of our people have nothing to show for their earnings."

The king was thoughtful for some time. Then he asked, "Why should so few men be able to acquire all the gold?"

"Because they know how," replied the chancellor. "One may not condemn a man for succeeding because he knows how. Neither may one with justice take away from a man what he has fairly earned, to give to men of less ability."

"But why," demanded the king, "should not all the people learn how to accumulate gold and therefore become themselves rich and prosperous?"

"Quite possible, Your Excellency, but who can teach them? Certainly not the priests, because they know naught of moneymaking."

"Who knows best in all our city how to become wealthy, chancellor?" asked the king.

"Thy question answers itself, Your Majesty. Who has amassed the greatest wealth in Babylon?"

"Well said, my able chancellor. It is Arkad. He is the richest man in Babylon. Bring him before me on the morrow."

Upon the following day, as the king had decreed, Arkad appeared before him, straight and sprightly despite his threescore years and ten.

"Arkad," spoke the King, "is it true thou art the richest man in Babylon?"

"So it is reported, Your Majesty, and no man disputes it."

"How becamest thou so wealthy?"

"By taking advantage of opportunities available to all citizens of our good city."

"Thou hadst nothing to start with?"

"Only a great desire for wealth. Besides this, nothing."

"Arkad," continued the king, "our city is in a very unhappy state because a few men know how to acquire wealth and therefore monopolize it, while the mass of our citizens lack the knowledge of how to keep any part of the gold they receive. It is my desire that Babylon be the wealthiest city in the world. Therefore it must be a city of many wealthy men. Therefore we must teach all the people how to acquire riches. Tell me, Arkad, is there any secret to acquiring wealth? Can it be taught?"

"It is practical, Your Majesty. That which one man knows can be taught to others."

The king's eyes glowed. "Arkad, thou speaketh the words I wish to hear. Wilt thou lend thyself to this great cause? Wilt thou teach thy knowledge to a school for teachers, each of whom shall teach others until there are enough trained to teach these truths to every worthy subject in my domain?"

Arkad bowed and said, "I am thy humble servant to command. Whatever knowledge I possess will I gladly give for the betterment of my fellowmen and the glory of my king. Let your good chancellor arrange for me a class of 100 men and I will teach to them those seven cures which did fatten my purse, than which there was none leaner in all Babylon."

A fortnight later, in compliance with the king's command, the chosen hundred assembled in the great hall of the Temple of Learning, seated upon colorful rings in a semicircle. Arkad sat beside a small taboret upon which smoked a sacred lamp sending forth a strange and pleasing odor.

"Behold the richest man in Babylon," whispered a student, nudging his neighbor as Arkad arose. "He is but a man even as the rest of us."

"As a dutiful subject of our great king," Arkad began, "I stand before you in his service. Because once I was a poor youth who did greatly desire gold, and because I found knowledge that enabled me to acquire it, he asks that I impart unto you my knowledge.

"I started my fortune in the humblest way. I had no advantage not enjoyed as fully by you and every citizen in Babylon.

"The first storehouse of my treasure was a well-worn purse. I loathed its useless emptiness. I desired it be round and full, clinking with the sound of gold. Therefore I sought every remedy for a lean purse. I found seven.

"To you, who are assembled before me, shall I explain the Seven Cures for a Lean Purse, which I do recommend to all men who desire much gold. Each day for seven days will I explain to you one of the seven remedies. Listen attentively to the knowledge that I will impart. Debate it with me. Discuss it among yourselves. Learn these lessons thoroughly, that ye may also plant in your own purse the seed of wealth.

"First must each of you start wisely to build a fortune of his own. Then wilt thou be competent, and only then, to teach these truths to others.

"I shall teach to you in simple ways how to fatten your purses. This is the first step leading to the temple of wealth, and no man may climb who cannot plant his feet firmly upon the first step. We shall now consider the first cure."

## The First Cure: Start thy purse to fattening.

Arkad addressed a thoughtful man in the second row. "My good friend, at what craft workest thou?"

"I," replied the man, "am a scribe, and carve records upon the clay tablets."

"Even at such labor did I myself earn my first coppers. Therefore thou hast the same opportunity to build a fortune."

He spoke to a florid-faced man farther back. "Pray tell also what dost thou to earn thy bread?"

"I," responded this man, "am a meat butcher. I do buy the goats the farmers raise and kill them and sell the meat to the housewives and the hides to the sandalmakers."

"Because thou dost also labor and earn, thou hast every advantage to succeed that I did possess."

In this way did Arkad proceed to find out how each man labored to earn his living. When he had done questioning them, he said, "Now, my students, ye can see that there are many trades and labors at which men may earn coins. Each of the ways of earning is a stream of gold from which the worker doth divert by his labors a portion to his own purse. Therefore into the purse of each of you flows a stream of coins large or small according to his ability. Is it not so?"

Thereupon they agreed that it was so. "Then," continued Arkad, "if each of you desireth to build for himself a fortune, is it not wise to start by utilizing that source of wealth which he already has established?"

To this they agreed. Then Arkad turned to a humble man who had declared himself an egg merchant. "If thou select one of thy baskets and put into it each morning ten eggs and take out from it each evening nine eggs, what will eventually happen?"

"It will become in time overflowing."

"Why?"

"Because each day I put in one more egg than I take out."

Arkad turned to the class with a smile. "Does any man here have a lean purse?" First they looked amused. Then they laughed. Lastly they waved their purses in jest.

"All right," he continued, "Now I shall tell thee the first remedy I learned to cure a lean purse. Do exactly as I have suggested to the egg merchant. For every ten coins thou placest within thy purse, take out for use but nine. Thy purse will start to fatten at once, and its increasing weight will feel good in thy hand and bring satisfaction to thy soul.

"Deride not what I say because of its simplicity. Truth is always simple. I told thee I would tell how built my fortune. This was my beginning. I, too, carried a lean purse and cursed it because there was naught within to satisfy my desires. But when I began to take out from my purse but nine parts of ten I put in, it began to fatten. So will thine.

"Now I will tell a strange truth, the reason for which I know not. When I ceased to pay out more than nine-tenths of my earnings, I managed to get along just as well. I was not shorter than before. Also, ere long, did coins come to me more easily than before. Surely it is a law of the gods that unto him who keepeth and spendeth not a certain part of all his earnings shall gold come more easily. Likewise, him whose purse is empty does gold avoid.

"Which desirest thou the most? Is it the gratification of thy desires of each day, a jewel, a bit of finery, better raiment, more food, things quickly gone and forgotten? Or is it substantial belongings, gold, lands, herds, merchandise, income-bringing investments? The coins thou takest from thy purse bring the first. The coins thou leavest within it will bring the latter.

"This, my students, was the first cure I did discover for my lean purse: for each ten coins I put in, to spend but nine. Debate this amongst yourselves. If any man proves it untrue, tell me upon the morrow, when we shall meet again."

## The Second Cure: Control thine expenditures.

"Some of your members, my students, have asked me this: how can a man keep one-tenth of all he earns in his purse when all the coins he earns are not enough for his necessary expenses?" So did Arkad address his students upon the second day. "Yesterday how many of thee carried lean purses?"

"All of us," answered the class.

"Yet you do not all earn the same. Some earn much more than others. Some have much larger families to support. Yet all purses were equally lean. Now I will tell thee an unusual truth about men and sons of men. It is this. That what each of us calls our 'necessary expenses' will always grow to equal our incomes unless we protest to the contrary.

"Confuse not the necessary expenses with thy desires. Each of you, together with your good families, have more desires than your earnings can gratify. Therefore are thine earnings spent to gratify these desires insofar as they will go. Still thou retainest many ungratified desires.

"All men are burdened with more desires than they can gratify. Because of my wealth thinkest thou I may gratify every desire? 'Tis a false idea. There are limits to my time. There are limits to my strength. There are limits to the distance I may travel. There are limits to what I may eat. There are limits to the zest with which I may enjoy.

"I say to you that just as weeds grow in a field wherever the farmer leaves space for their roots, even so freely do desires grow in men whenever there is a possibility of their being gratified. Thy desires are a multitude, and those that thou mayest gratify are but few.

"Study thoughtfully thy accustomed habits of living. Herein may be most often found certain accepted expenses that may wisely be reduced or eliminated. Let thy motto be: 100 percent of appreciated value demanded for each coin spent. Therefore engrave upon the clay each thing for which thou desireth to spend. Select those that are necessary and others that are possible through the expenditure of nine-tenths of thy income. Cross out the rest and consider them but a part of that great multitude of desires that must go unsatisfied, and regret them not.

"Budget then thy necessary expenses. Touch not the one-tenth that is fattening thy purse. Let this be thy great desire that is being fulfilled. Keep working with thy budget, keep adjusting it to help thee. Make it thy first assistant in defending thy fattening purse."

Hereupon one of the students, wearing a robe of red and gold, arose and said, "I am a free man. I believe that it is my right to enjoy the good things of life. Therefore do I rebel against the slavery of a budget which determines just how much I may spend and for what. I feel it would take much pleasure from my life and make me little more than a pack ass to carry a burden."

To him Arkad replied, "Who, my friend, would determine thy budget?"

"I would make it for myself," responded the protesting one.

"In that case, were a pack ass to budget his burden, would he include therein jewels and rugs and heavy bars of gold? Not so. He would include hay and grain and a bag of water for the desert trail. The purpose of a budget is to help thy purse to fatten. It is to assist thee to have thy necessities and, insofar as attainable, thy other desires.

It is to enable thee to realize thy most cherished desires by defending them from thy casual wishes. Like a bright light in a dark cave thy budget shows up the leaks from thy purse and enables thee to stop them and control thine expenditures for definite and gratifying purposes.

"This, then, is the second cure for a lean purse: budget thy expenses that thou mayest have coins to pay for thy necessities, to pay for thy enjoyments, and to gratify thy worthwhile desires without spending more than nine-tenths of thine earnings."

## The Third Cure: make thy gold multiply.

"Behold, thy lean purse is fattening. Thou hast disciplined thyself to leave therein one-tenth of all thou earnest. Thou hast controlled thine expenditures to protect thy growing treasure.

"Next, we will consider means to put thy treasure to labor and to increase. Gold in a purse is gratifying to own and satisfieth a miserly soul, but earns nothing. The gold we may retain from our earnings is but the start. The earnings it will make shall build our fortunes." So spoke Arkad upon the third day to his class.

"How, therefore, may we put our gold to work? My first investment was unfortunate, for I lost all. Its tale I will relate later. My first profitable investment was a loan I made to a man named Agger, a shieldmaker. Once each year did he buy large shipments of bronze brought from across the sea to use in his trade. Lacking sufficient capital to pay the merchants, he would borrow from those who had extra coins. He was an honorable man. His borrowing he would repay, together with a liberal rental, as he sold his shields.

"Each time I loaned to him, I loaned back also the rental he had paid to me. Therefore not only did my capital increase, but its earnings likewise increased. Most gratifying was it to have these sums return to my purse.

"I tell you, my students, a man's wealth is not in the coins he carries in his purse; it is the income he buildeth, the golden stream that continually floweth into his purse and keepeth it always bulging. That is what every man desireth. That is what thou, each one of thee, desirest; an income that continueth to come whether thou work or travel.

"Great income I have acquired. So great that I am called a very rich man. My loans to Agger were my first training in profitable investment. Gaining wisdom from this experience, I extended my loans and investments as my capital increased. From a few sources at first, from many sources later, flowed into my purse a golden stream of wealth available for such wise uses as I should decide.

"Behold, from my humble earnings I have begotten a hoard of golden slaves, each laboring and earning more gold. As they labored for me, so their children also labored and their children's children, until great was the income from their combined efforts. Gold increaseth rapidly when making reasonable earnings, as thou wilt see from the following.

"A farmer, when his first son was born, took ten pieces of silver to a moneylender and asked him to keep it on rental for his son until he became twenty years of age.

This the moneylender did, and agreed the rental should be one-fourth of its value each four years. The farmer asked, because this sum he had set aside as belonging to his son, that the rental be added to the principal.

"When the boy had reached the age of twenty years, the farmer again went to the moneylender to inquire about the silver. The moneylender explained that because this sum had been increased by compound interest, the original ten pieces of silver had now grown to thirty and one-half pieces. The farmer was well pleased and because the son did not need the coins, he left them with the moneylender.

"When the son became fifty years of age, the father meantime having passed to the other world, the moneylender paid the son in settlement 167 pieces of silver. Thus in fifty years had the investment multiplied itself at rental almost seventeen times.

"This, then, is the third cure for a lean purse: to put each coin to laboring that it may reproduce its kind, even as the flocks of the field, and help bring to thee income, a stream of wealth that shall flow constantly into thy purse."

## The Fourth Cure:
## Guard thy treasures from loss.

"Misfortune loves a shining mark. Gold in a man's purse must be guarded with firmness, else it be lost. Thus it is wise that we must first secure small amounts and learn to protect them before the gods entrust us with larger." So spoke Arkad upon the fourth day to his class.

"Every owner of gold is tempted by opportunities whereby it would seem that he could make large sums by its investment in most plausible projects.

Often friends and relatives are eagerly entering such investment and urge him to follow.

"The first sound principle of investment is security for thy principal. Is it wise to be intrigued by larger earnings when thy principal may be lost? I say not. The penalty of risk is probable loss. Study carefully, before parting with thy treasure, each assurance that it may be safely reclaimed. Be not misled by thine own romantic desires to make wealth rapidly.

"Before thou loan it to any man, assure thyself of his ability to repay and his reputation for doing, so that thou mayest not unwittingly be making him a present of thy hard-earned treasure.

"Before thou entrust it as an investment in any field, acquaint thyself with the dangers which may beset it. My own first investment was a tragedy to me at the time. The guarded savings of a year I did entrust to a brickmaker named Azmur, who was traveling over the far seas, and in Tyre agreed to buy for me the rare jewels of the Phoenicians. These we would sell upon his return and divide the profits.

"The Phoenicians were scoundrels and sold him bits of glass. My treasure was lost. Today my training would show to me at once the folly of entrusting a brickmaker to buy jewels. Therefore do I advise thee from the wisdom of my experiences: be not too confident of thine own wisdom in entrusting thy treasures to the possible pitfalls of investments. Better by far to consult the wisdom of those experienced in handling money for profit. Such advice is freely given for the asking and may readily possess a value equal in gold to the sum thou considerest investing. In truth, such is its actual value if it save thee from loss.

"This, then, is the fourth cure for a lean purse, and of great importance if it prevent thy purse from being emptied once it has become well filled. Guard thy treasure from loss by investing only where thy principal is safe, where it may be reclaimed if desirable, and where thou wilt not fail to collect a fair rental. Consult with wise men. Secure the advice of those experienced in the profitable handling of gold. Let their wisdom protect thy treasure from unsafe investments."

## The Fifth Cure:
## Make of thy dwelling a profitable investment.

"If a man setteth aside nine parts of his earnings upon which to live and enjoy life, and if any part of this nine parts he can turn into a profitable investment without detriment to his well-being, then so much faster will his treasures grow." So spake Arkad to his class at their fifth lesson.

"All too many of our men of Babylon do raise their families in unseemly quarters. They do pay to exacting landlords liberal rentals for rooms where their wives have not a spot to raise the blooms that gladden a woman's heart and their children have no place to play their games except in the unclean alleys.

"No man's family can fully enjoy life unless they do have a plot of ground wherein children can play in the clean earth and where the wife may raise not only blossoms but good rich herbs to feed her family.

"To a man's heart it brings gladness to eat the figs from his own trees and the grapes of his own vines. To own his own domicile, and to have it a place he is proud to care for, putteth confidence in his heart and greater effort behind all his endeavors. Therefore do I recommend that every man own the roof that sheltereth him and his.

"Nor is it beyond the ability of any well-intentioned man to own his home. Hath not our great king so widely extended the walls of Babylon that within them much land is now unused and may be purchased at sums most reasonable? Also I say to you, my students, that the moneylenders gladly consider the desires of men who seek homes and land for their families. Readily mayest thou borrow to pay the brickmaker and the builder for such commendable purposes, if thou canst show a reasonable portion of the necessary sum which thou thyself hast provided for the purpose. Then, when the house be built, thou canst pay the moneylender with the same regularity as thou didst pay the landlord. Because each payment will reduce thy indebtedness to the moneylender, a few years will satisfy his loan.

"Then will thy heart be glad because thou wilt own in thine own right a valuable property, and thy only cost will be the king's taxes. Also wilt thy good wife go more often to the river to wash thy robes, that each time returning she may bring a goatskin of water to pour upon the growing things.

"Thus come many blessings to the man who owneth his own house, and greatly will it reduce his cost of living, making available more of his earnings for pleasures and the gratification of his desires. This then, is the fifth cure for a lean purse. Own thine own home."

## The Sixth Cure: Ensure a future income.

"The life of every man proceedeth from his childhood to his old age. This is the path of life, and no man may deviate from it unless the gods call him prematurely to the world beyond. Therefore do I say that it behooves a man to make preparation for a suitable income in the days to come, when he is no longer young, and to make preparations for his family should he be no longer with them to comfort and support them. This lesson shall instruct thee in providing a full purse when time has made thee less able to learn." So Arkad addressed his class upon the sixth day.

"The man who, because of his understanding of the laws of wealth, acquireth a growing surplus, should give thought to those future days. He should plan certain investments or provisions that may endure safely for many years, yet will be available when the time arrives which he has so wisely anticipated.

"There are diverse ways by which a man may provide with safety for his future. He may provide a hiding place and there bury a secret treasure. Yet no matter with what skill it be hidden, it may nevertheless become the loot of thieves. For this reason I recommend not this plan.

"A man may buy houses or lands for this purpose. If wisely chosen as to their usefulness and value in the future, they are permanent in their value and their earnings, or their sale will provide well for his purpose.

"A man may loan a small sum to the moneylender and increase it at regular periods. The rental which the moneylender adds to this will largely add to its increase. I do know a sandalmaker named Ansan, who explained to me not long ago that each week for eight years he had deposited with his moneylender two pieces of silver. The moneylender had but recently given him an accounting over which he greatly rejoiced. The total of his small deposits with their rental at the customary rate of one-fourth their value for each four years, had now become 1040 pieces of silver.

"I did gladly encourage him further by demonstrating to him with my knowledge of the numbers that in twelve years more, if he would keep his regular deposits of but two pieces of silver each week, the moneylender would then owe him 4000 pieces of silver, a worthy competence for the rest of his life.

"Surely, when such a small payment made with regularity doth produce such profitable results, no man can afford not to insure a treasure for his old age and the protection of his family, no matter how prosperous his business and his investments may be.

"I would that I might say more about this. In my mind rests a belief that some day wise, thinking men will devise a plan to insure against death whereby many men pay in but a trifling sum regularly, the aggregate making a handsome sum for the family of each member who passeth to the beyond. This do I see as something desirable and which I could highly recommend, but today it is not possible, because it must reach beyond the life of any man or any partnership to operate. It must be as stable as the king's throne.

"Someday do I feel that such a plan shall come to pass and be a great blessing to many men, because even the first small payment will make available a snug fortune for the family of a member should he pass on.

"But because we live in our own day and not in the days which are to come, must we take advantage of those means and ways of accomplishing our purposes. Therefore do I recommend to all men, that they, by wise and well-thought-out methods, do provide against a lean purse in their mature years. For a lean purse to a man no longer able to earn or to a family without its head is a sore tragedy. This, then, is the sixth cure for a lean purse: provide in advance for the needs of thy growing age and the protection of thy family."

## The Seventh Cure:
## Increase thine ability to earn.

"This day do I speak to thee, my students, of one of the most vital remedies for a lean purse. Yet I will talk not of gold but of yourselves, of the men beneath the robes of many colors who do sit before me. I will talk to you of those things within the minds and lives of men which do work for or against their success." So did Arkad address his class upon the seventh day.

"Not long ago came to me a young man seeking to borrow. When I questioned him the cause of his necessity, he complained that his earnings were insufficient to pay his expenses. Thereupon I explained to him, this being the case, he was a poor customer for the moneylender, as he possessed no surplus earning capacity to repay the loan. 'What you need, young man,' I told him, 'is to earn more coins. What dost thou to increase thy capacity to earn?'

"'All that I can do' he replied. 'Six times within two moons have I approached my master to request my pay be increased, but without success. No man can go oftener than that.'

"We may smile at his simplicity, yet he did possess one of the vital requirements to increase his earnings. Within him was a strong desire to earn more, a proper and commendable desire. Preceding accomplishment must be desire. Thy desires must be strong and definite. General desires are but weak longings. For a man to wish to be rich is of little purpose. For a man to desire five pieces of gold is a tangible desire, which he can press to fulfilment. After he has backed his desire for five pieces of gold with strength of purpose to secure it, next he can find similar ways to obtain ten pieces, and then twenty pieces, and later 1000 pieces and, behold, he has become wealthy. In learning to secure his one definite small desire, he hath trained himself to secure a larger one. This is the process by which wealth is accumulated, first in small sums, then in larger ones as a man learns and becomes more capable.

"Desires must be simple and definite. They defeat their own purpose should they be too many, too confusing, or beyond a man's training to accomplish.

"As a man perfecteth himself in his calling, even so doth his ability to earn increase. In those days when I was a humble scribe carving upon the clay for a few coppers each day, I observed that other workers did more than I and were paid more.

"Therefore did I determine that I would be exceeded by none. Nor did it take long for me to discover the reason for their greater success. More interest in my work, more concentration upon my task, more persistence in my effort, and, behold, few men could carve more tablets in a day than I. With reasonable promptness my increased skill was rewarded, nor was it necessary for me to go six times to my master to request recognition.

"The more of wisdom we know, the more we may earn. That man who seeks to learn more of his craft shall be richly rewarded. If he is an artisan, he may seek to learn the methods and the tools of those most skillful in the same line. If he laboreth at the law or at healing, he may consult and exchange knowledge with others of his calling. If he be a merchant, he may continually seek better goods that can be purchased at lower prices.

"Always do the affairs of man change and improve because keen-minded men seek greater skill, that they may better serve those upon whose patronage they depend. Therefore I urge all men to be in the front rank of progress and not to stand still, lest they be left behind.

"Many things come to make a man's life rich with gainful experiences. Such things as the following a man must do if he respects himself. He must pay his debts with all the promptness within his power, not purchasing that for which he is unable to pay. He must take care of his family, that they may think and speak well of him. He must make a will of record that, in case the gods call him, proper and honorable division of his property be accomplished.

"He must have compassion upon those who are injured and smitten by misfortune, and aid them within reasonable limits. He must do deeds of thoughtfulness to those dear to him.

"Thus the seventh and last remedy for a lean purse is to cultivate thine own powers, to study and become wiser, to become more skillful, to so act as to respect thyself. Thereby shalt thou acquire confidence in thyself to achieve thy carefully considered desires.

"These, then, are the Seven Cures for a Lean Purse, which, out of the experience of a long and successful life, I do urge for all men who desire wealth.

"There is more gold in Babylon, my students, than thou dreamest of. There is abundance for all. Go thou forth and practice these truths, that thou mayest prosper and grow wealthy, as is thy right. Go thou forth and teach these truths, that every honorable subject of his majesty may also share liberally in the ample wealth of our beloved city."

# ❧ Dan ☙

In our story, Babylon, the richest city during that time, is experiencing an economic downturn. Sound familiar? Sure, but remember: ideas taught in *The Richest Man in Babylon* held strong through the Great Depression, and will hold true now.

In Babylon, the downturn was because a few rich men acquired the wealth of the city and left the majority of the citizens in poverty. Because of this, the good King Sargon was very worried and ordered the royal chancellor to bring Arkad to him, because he believed that he knew the answers to the city's problem.

The king asked Arkad what the secret to acquiring wealth was and whether or not it could be taught to others. Of course, you and I know that it can be taught. Arkad came before a class of 100 men assembled in the great hall of the Temple of Learning, and we can learn a lot from him, even though the great hall of the Temple of Learning is now the book you are reading.

Let's go through the Seven Cures and see how they apply to your life today. Arkad stated the first cure to a lean purse, which is *start thy purse to fattening.* He asked some of the men what they did for a living. He turned to an egg merchant and asked him, if he put in ten eggs in his basket each morning but took out only nine, what would happen? The egg merchant answered that it would eventually overflow.

Arkad smiled to the class and said that he just taught the first remedy to a lean purse. For every ten coins that you place in your purse, take out only nine. Pretty soon, the purse will start to feel heavy, and you'll start to feel rich.

In our day and age, we don't exactly walk around with gold coins in our purses or pockets, and if we had pockets full of quarters, we'd feel strange instead of wealthy. So how can we apply the first cure?

One way is to put $100 bill in your wallet. Carry around what to you is a fairly significant amount of money. If $100 is nothing to you, then make it $1000. Of course, don't carry more than you can afford to lose if your wallet gets left in a restaurant, but carry enough so that when you open your wallet, you can start to feel wealthy. So the next time you go to the bank, take out a $100 bill, and keep it in your purse or wallet. Don't break it. Don't spend it. Just put it in your wallet and look at it. Every time you put some money in the bank, try to take out a tenth of it in cash and carry it around.

If you can't take out a whole tenth, take some money out, even if it's only $20, and keep it in your wallet. Pretty soon your wallet is going to be pretty full. You'll start to see the first cure in action.

Let's move onto the second cure. What if you can't even afford one-tenth of your earnings for saving? The next day some of the class asked Arkad how they could save one-tenth of their earnings if they didn't even make enough for their necessary expenses. Arkad told them not to confuse necessary expenses with desires.

We all have more desires than our income can gratify. He told the group that they should learn to live simply and should budget their earnings to their necessary expenses. Arkad said, "The second cure is budget thy expenses, that thou mayest have coins to pay for thy necessities, to pay for thy enjoyments, and to gratify thy worthwhile desires without spending more than nine-tenths of thine earnings."

What does that mean for us in modern times? It's what author David Bach termed the Latte Factor. The Latte Factor is the amount of money that each one of us wastes on insignificant little things we want rather than on necessary expenses. The best way to find out what is a necessary expense and what is not is to track your spending for a full week. This simple exercise can be life-changing.

So in your journal for the next week, write down every single thing you buy and its cost, big or small. It might be a pain to do, but it will be worth it. Then at the end of the week, add up all the things you spent money on that weren't essential. What if you took that money and saved it, leaving the other nine-tenths of your income for actual expenses?

Let's move onto the third cure. Arkad told the class that they should put their treasure or savings to labor and make it multiply. They must put it into an investment, because a man's wealth is not in the coins he carries in his purse, but it is the income that he builds.

We've all seen this principle in action in the modern world, haven't we? Real wealth has nothing to do with the car you drive, the clothes that you wear, or the purse that you carry, or anything else that relates to the amount of money you have to spend.

Instead, real wealth comes from the income stream you build. If you don't have your money working for you to make more money, you're not really wealthy. That's a powerful lesson that applies both today and in the ancient times of Babylon.

Arkad stated it this way, "Put each coin to laboring, that it may be reproduce its kind even as the flocks of the field and help bring to the income a stream of wealth that shall flow constantly into thy purse."

Let's talk a bit about how to get that gold in your bank account to reproduce. The IRS divides income into two basic categories: *earned income*, such as from a job, and *passive income*. We've already talked about keeping part of what you earn for yourself, but the third cure is saying that you need to have some kind of passive income or portfolio income stream too.

Passive income, according to the IRS, is income that comes to you from business activities that you don't materially participate in. If you write a book and get royalties from it, that income is considered passive, because you don't have to rewrite the book each time to earn the money. You do it once, and you earn money over and over and over again.

Here are some other examples of passive income: rental from property, residuals or repeated regular income earned by a salesperson, the income that comes from your down line in a network marketing company, affiliate income or licensing of intellectual property, and franchising fees. Another form of passive income is portfolio income, which comes from your investments.

Now it's time for another exercise. Write down any passive income streams that you might have already. Are there any additional ones that interest you?

Let's move onto the fourth cure. On the fourth day, Arkad explained to his class that they should study carefully how business flows before making an investment. They must insure their investment from risk of loss. In modern terms, it's called *not risking your principal.*

Arkad told the class not to be fooled by the idea of earning a large amount of money, but instead to consult the wisdom of those who are experienced in handling money for profit. "Guard thy treasure from loss by investing only where thy principal is safe, where it may be reclaimed if desirable, and where thou wilt not fail to collect a fair rental. Consult with wise men. Secure the advice of those experienced in the profitable handling of gold. Let their wisdom protect thy treasure from unsafe investments."

It's pretty clear how this relates to our modern times. In order to wisely and safely invest your money, you need to learn how to do it from an expert; otherwise you're more likely to lose your principal investment. It's a good idea to sit down in person and have an honest conversation with an expert about your specific situation. The meeting may not be free, but it will save you a lot of money in the long run.

When you're seeking the advice of wise men or women who are experienced in the profitable handling of gold, you need to make sure that you choose wisely. We've all heard news stories of people who have been swindled out of their life savings by unscrupulous advisors.

Here are some key points to consider. First, don't be dazzled by promises of high returns. If it seems too good to be true, it probably is. A good financial advisor wants to teach you. If he or she is not willing to explain something to you in clear and understandable terms, then you need to go somewhere else.

Second, an advisor should always disclose his or her fees and explain to you why the fee is what it is. The advisor should give you a range of options, and then recommend which is best for you, but the advisor needs to explain why he or she is making that recommendation.

Third, and most importantly, you have to trust the integrity of your investment advisor before you do any business with him or her. It's the foundation of your relationship. Trust your instincts, and if something feels funny, then move on.

Let's move on to applying the fifth cure. On the fifth day of class, Arkad suggested that the students needed to own their own homes. He explained that if they choose to rent a room or a house, their families would not be at ease. He also stated that a man who has his own domicile will receive many blessings and will reduce his cost of living. Lastly, he will satisfy his desires.

Overall, in the long run, real estate is always a good investment. A we all know, the market has ups and downs, but over time, real estate generally increases in value. But you have to be careful. As we learned in the previous cure, you have to take the advice of an expert in real estate. You need to make sure that you work with someone who has your best interest at heart, and who isn't only interested in making a commission.

Here are five ways to find money for your down payment. Number one: open a savings account just for your new home down payment, and every time you get a few extra dollars, make sure you put them in this account. Number two: earmark your annual bonuses and raises for your new home down payment account.

Number three: if necessary, look into cashing in the value of your life insurance policies. Many times you can cash out your old whole-life policies and replace them with less expensive term policies. You'll still have coverage, but more importantly, you'll have extra money that you can use towards your home down payment.

Number four: consider using your tax-shelter accounts at work. Many of these offer special privileges that will allow you to take money out for your down payment. Number five: secure gifts from your friends and family members. If you have a friend or family member who wants to loan you the money to put down on your home, and you tie up a loan agreement, the bank will take that into consideration and will provide you with a mortgage.

Once you make a commitment to becoming a homeowner or even to buying a bigger and better home, you can always find the money. The most important thing to do is to have the goal and to understand the importance of building equity in your home that will help you win the great financial game of life.

Besides the financial aspect of owning your own home, there is another element at work here. Arkad talks about the psychological feeling that you get from owing your own home, but you're not going to have that feeling of security if you have a huge mortgage. That's why you need to focus on owning your home, not paying a mortgage on it.

There are audio programs that will show you how to pay off your mortgage in as few as five to ten years. Once you've followed the steps and paid off your mortgage, you truly will own your home, and you will get the psychological sense of freedom and security that comes from that.

On the sixth day, Arkad told the class that the sixth cure is, "Provide in advance for the needs of thy growing age and the protection of thy family."

This is another area that's really relevant today. People are living longer than ever before. Often we retire at sixty-five or seventy years of age and then go on to live another ten to twenty years. We have to make sure that we have enough income to last that long, and we have to plan in case we get sick and can't work.

Have you decided at what age you want to retire? Do you know what you want to do with your days? Have you put a savings plan in place? Do you even know how much money you're going to need each month? What is your insurance like? Have you made plans for if you get ill or incapacitated?

The Social Security website (www.ssa.gov/retire2) offers a useful planner to help you plan your finances so that you can be prepared for retirement. You can find your retirement age and use their estimator to find out how much money you'll be earning depending on what age you retire. It's a really useful tool even if you aren't close to retiring.

By taking a solid look at what you're going to need in the future, you can take the steps to build a future income that can support that lifestyle.

Let's move on to the seventh and final cure for a lean purse. On the last day, Arkad talked about some other things that are important for making your life rich. You have to pay off your debts as promptly has possible and not buy things you can't afford. Take care of your family, so they'll think and speak well of you. Make a will so that a proper and honorable distribution of your property can be accomplished, and have compassion for those less fortunate, and help them out within reasonable limits.

These are truly timeless qualities, aren't they? Be a good person. Be responsible. Help others. Arkad told the class that the seventh cure for a lean purse is "to cultivate thine own powers to study and become wiser, to become more skillful, to so act as to respect thyself."

That's exactly what you're doing now, isn't it? You're learning new things. In addition to studying the laws of wealth building, though, you also need to cultivate some new skills that can actually earn you more money. Remember, in order to earn more, you have to know how to solve problems that people are willing to pay to have solved.

How does this apply to you? Get your journal, and take some time to reflect on things you could learn that would enhance your ability to earn more money. Maybe you've been meaning to take a computer class. Would becoming bilingual help you earn more? What can you learn that can translate into more gold in your purse?

The most important thing to remember from this chapter is Arkad's comment that there is more than enough gold in Babylon. Regardless of the economic conditions, you can still use the Seven Cures for a Lean Purse to become wealthy.

## Babylon Builder

This was an information-packed chapter. We learned about the Seven Cures for a Lean Purse. We learned more about why it's important to keep 10 percent of what you earn and to live on the remaining 90 percent. You learned about the Latte Factor and how to identify a want versus a need. You learned how to find a good financial advisor.

We talked about the different kinds of passive income in today's world, and we learned five ways to find a down payment for your house. You discovered that if you learn more, you'll earn more.

For action steps, you started tracking your expenses. You made an appointment to meet with a financial advisor and started planning for your retirement. Finally, you identified something new that you can learn to increase your earning power.

If you haven't done these things yet, what are you waiting for? Make sure you do them before you move on to the next chapter and learn about the Goddess of Good Luck.

# FIVE
# Meet the Goddess
# of Good Luck

*If a man be lucky, there is no foretelling*
*the possible extent of his good fortune.*
*Pitch him into the Euphrates, and like as not*
*he will swim out with a pearl in his hand.*
BABYLONIAN PROVERB

The desire to be lucky is universal. It was just as strong in the breasts of men 4,000 years ago in ancient Babylon as it is in the hearts of men today. We all hope to be favored by the whimsical Goddess of Good Luck. Is there some way we can meet her and attract, not only her favorable attention, but her generous favors? Is there a way to attract good luck?

That is just what the men of ancient Babylon wished to know. It is exactly what they decided to find out. They were shrewd men and keen thinkers. That explains why their city became the richest and most powerful city of their time.

In that distant past, they had no schools or colleges. Nevertheless, they had a center of learning, and a very practical one it was. Among the towered buildings in Babylon was one that ranked in importance with the palace of the king, the Hanging Gardens, and the temples of the gods. You will find scant mention of it in the history books, more likely no mention at all, yet it exerted a powerful influence upon the thought of that time.

This building was the Temple of Learning, where the wisdom of the past was expounded by voluntary teachers and where subjects of popular interest were discussed in open forums. Within its walls all men met as equals. The humblest of slaves could dispute with impunity the opinions of a prince of the royal house.

Among the many who frequented the Temple of Learning was a wise rich man named Arkad, called the richest man in Babylon. He had his own special hall, where almost any evening a large group of men, some old, some very young, but mostly middle-aged, gathered to discuss and argue interesting subjects. Suppose we listen in to see whether they knew how to attract good luck.

The sun had just set like a great, red ball of fire shining through the haze of desert dust when Arkad strolled to his accustomed platform. Already full fourscore men were awaiting his arrival, reclining on their small rugs spread upon the floor. More were still arriving.

"What shall we discuss this night?" Arkad inquired.

After a brief hesitation, a tall cloth weaver addressed him, arising, as was the custom. "I have a subject I would like to hear discussed, yet hesitate to offer lest it seem ridiculous to you, Arkad, and my good friends here."

Upon being urged to offer it, both by Arkad and by calls from the others, he continued, "This day I have been lucky, for I have found a purse in which there are pieces of gold. To continue to be lucky is my great desire. Feeling that all men share with me this desire, I do suggest we debate how to attract good luck, that we may discover ways it can be enticed to one."

"A most interesting subject has been offered," Arkad commented, "one most worthy of our discussion. To some men, good luck bespeaks but a chance happening that, like an accident, may befall one without purpose or reason. Others do believe that the instigator of all good fortune is our most bounteous goddess Ashtar, ever anxious to reward with generous gifts those who please her. Speak up, my friends. What say you? Shall we seek to find if there be means by which good luck may be enticed to visit each and all of us?"

"Yea, yea, and much of it," responded the growing group of eager listeners.

Thereupon Arkad continued, "To start our discussion, let us first hear from those among us who have enjoyed experiences similar to that of the cloth weaver in finding or receiving, without effort upon their part, valuable treasures or jewels."

There was a pause in which all looked about expecting someone to reply, but no one did.

"What, no one?" Arkad said. "Then rare indeed must be this kind of good luck. Who now will offer a suggestion as to where we shall continue our search?"

"That I will do," spoke a well-robed young man, arising. "When a man speaketh of luck, is it not natural that his thoughts turn to the gaming tables? Is it not there we find many men courting the favor of the goddess in hope she will bless them with rich winnings?"

As he resumed his seat a voice called, "Do not stop. Continue thy story. Tell us, didst thou find favor with the goddess at the gaming tables? Did she turn the cubes with red side up so thou filledst thy purse at the dealer's expense, or did she permit the blue sides to come up so the dealer raked in thy hard-earned pieces of silver?"

The young man joined the good-natured laughter, then replied, "I am not averse to admitting she seemed not to know I was even there, but how about the rest of you? Have you found her waiting about such places to roll the cubes in your favor? We are eager to hear as well as to learn."

"A wise start," broke in Arkad. "We meet here to consider all sides of each question. To ignore the gaming table would be to overlook an instinct common to most men, the love of taking a chance with a small amount of silver in the hope of winning much gold."

"That doth remind me of the races but yesterday," called out another listener. "If the goddess frequents the gaming tables, certainly she doth not overlook the races where the gilded chariots and the foaming horses offer far more excitement. Tell us honestly, Arkad, did she whisper to you to place your bet upon those grey horses from Nineveh yesterday?

"I was standing just behind thee and could scarce believe my ears when I heard thee place thy bet upon the greys. Thou knowest as well as any of us that no team in all Assyria can beat our beloved bays in a fair race.

"Did the goddess whisper in thine ear to bet upon the greys because at the last turn the inside black would stumble and so interfere with our bays that the greys would win the race and score an unearned victory?"

Arkad smiled indulgently at the banter. "What reason have we to feel the good goddess would take that much interest in any man's bet upon a horse race? To me, she is a goddess of love and dignity, whose pleasure it is to aid those who are in need and to reward those who are deserving. I look to find her, not at the gaming tables or the races where men lose more gold than they win, but in other places, where the doings of men are more worthwhile and more worthy of reward.

"In tilling the soil, in honest trading, in all of man's occupations, there is opportunity to make a profit upon his efforts and his transactions. Perhaps not all the time will he be rewarded, because sometimes his judgment may be faulty, and other times the winds and the weather may defeat his efforts. Yet if he persists, he may usually expect to realize his profit. This is so because the chances of profit are always in his favor.

"But when a man playeth the games, the situation is reversed, for the chances of profit are always against him and always in favor of the gamekeeper. The game is so arranged that it will always favor the keeper. It is his business, at which he plans to make a liberal profit for himself from the coins bet by the players. Few players realize how certain are the gamekeeper's profits and how uncertain are their own chances to win.

"For example, let us consider wagers placed upon the cube. Each time it is cast, we bet which side will be uppermost. If it be the red side, the game master pays to us four times our bet, but if any other of the five sides comes uppermost, we lose our bet. Thus the figures show that for each cast we have five chances to lose, but because the red pays four for one, we have four chances to win. In a night's play the game master can expect to keep for his profit one-fifth of all the coins wagered. Can a man expect to win more than occasionally against odds so arranged that he should lose one-fifth of all his bets?"

"Yet some men do win large sums at times," volunteered one of the listeners.

"Quite so, they do," Arkad continued. "Realizing this, the question comes to me whether money secured in such ways brings permanent value to those who are thus lucky. Among my acquaintances are many of the successful men of Babylon, yet among them I am unable to name a single one who started his success from such a source.

"You who are gathered here tonight know many more of our substantial citizens. To me, it would be of much interest to learn how many of our successful citizens can credit the gaming tables with their start to success. Suppose each of you tell of those you know. What say you?"

After a prolonged silence, a wag ventured, "Would thine inquiry include the gamekeepers?"

"If you can think of no one else," Arkad responded. "If not one of you can think of anyone else, then how about yourselves? Are there any consistent winners with us who hesitate to advise such a source for their incomes?"

His challenge was answered by a series of groans from the rear taken up and spread amid much laughter. "It would seem we are not seeking good luck in such places as the goddess frequents," he continued. "Therefore let us explore other fields. We have not found it in picking up lost wallets. Neither have we found it haunting the gaming tables. As to the races, I must confess to have lost far more coins there than I have ever won.

"No, suppose we consider our trades and businesses. Is it not natural, if we conclude a profitable transaction, to consider it not good luck but a just reward for our efforts? I am inclined to think we may be overlooking the gifts of the goddess. Perhaps she really does assist us when we do not appreciate her generosity. Who can suggest further discussion?"

Thereupon an elderly merchant arose, smoothing his genteel white robe. "With thy permission, most honorable Arkad and my friends, I offer a suggestion. If, as you have said, we take credit to our own industry and ability for our business success, why not consider the successes we almost enjoyed but which escaped us, happenings which would have been most profitable? They would have been rare examples of good luck if they had actually happened. Because they were not brought to fulfillment, we cannot consider them as our just rewards. Surely many men here have such experiences to relate."

"Here is a wise approach," Arkad approved. "Who among you have had good luck within your grasp, only to see it escape?"

Many hands were raised, among them that of the merchant. Arkad motioned to him to speak. "As you suggested this approach, we should like to hear first from you."

"I will gladly relate a tale," he resumed, "that doth illustrate how closely unto a man good luck may approach and how blindly he may permit it to escape, much to his loss and later regret.

"Many years ago, when I was a young man, just married and well-started to earning, my father did come one day and urge most strongly that I enter into an investment. The son of one of his good friends had taken notice of a barren tract of land not far beyond the outer walls of our city. It lay high above the canal, where no water could reach it.

"The son of my father's friend devised a plan to purchase this land, build three large water wheels that could be operated by oxen and thereby raise the life-giving waters to the fertile soil. This accomplished, he planned to divide it into small tracts and sell to the residents of the city for herb patches.

"The son of my father's friend did not possess sufficient gold to complete such an undertaking. Like myself, he was a young man earning a fair sum. His father, like mine, was a man of large family and small means.

"He therefore decided to interest a group of men to enter the enterprise with him. The group was to comprise twelve, each of whom must be a money earner and agree to pay one-tenth of his earnings into the enterprise until the land was made ready for sale. All would then share justly in the profits in proportion to their investment.

"'Thou, my son,' bespoke my father unto me, 'art now in thy young manhood. It is my deep desire that thou begin the building of a valuable estate for myself, that thou mayest become respected among men. I desire to see thee profit from a knowledge of the thoughtless mistakes of thy father.'

"'This do I most ardently desire, my father,' I replied.

"'Then this do I advise. Do what I should have done at thy age. From thine earnings keep out one-tenth to put into favorable investments. With this one-tenth of thine earnings and what it will also earn, thou canst, before thou art my age, accumulate for thyself a valuable estate.'

"'Thy words are words of wisdom, my father. Greatly do I desire riches. Yet there are many uses to which my earnings are called. Therefore do I hesitate to do as thou dost advise. I am young. There is plenty of time.' So I thought at thy age, yet behold, many years have passed, and I have not yet made the beginning. 'We live in a different age, my father. I shall avoid thy mistakes.'

"'Opportunity stands before thee, my son. It is offering a chance that may lead to wealth. I beg of thee, do not delay. Go upon the morrow to the son of my friend and bargain with him to pay 10 percent of thine earnings into this investment. Go promptly upon the morrow. Opportunity waits for no man. Today it is here; soon it is gone. Therefore delay not.'

"In spite of the advice of my father, I did hesitate. There were beautiful new robes just brought by the tradesmen from the East, robes of such richness and beauty my good wife and I felt we must each possess one. Should I agree to pay one-tenth of my earnings into the enterprise, we must deprive ourselves of these and other pleasures we dearly desired. I delayed making a decision until it was too late, much to my subsequent regret. The enterprise did prove to be more profitable than any man had prophesied. This is my tale, showing how I did permit good luck to escape."

"In this tale we see how good luck waits to come to that man who accepts opportunity," commented a swarthy man of the desert. "To the building of an estate there must always be the beginning. That start may be a few pieces of gold or silver which a man diverts from his earnings to his first investment. I myself am the owner of many herds. The start of my herds I did begin when I was a mere boy and did purchase with one piece of silver a young calf. This, being the beginning of my wealth, was of great importance to me.

"To take his first start to building an estate is as good luck as can come to any man. With all men, that first step, which changes them from men who earn from their own labor to men who draw dividends from the earnings of their gold, is important. Some, fortunately, take it when young and thereby outstrip in financial success those who do take it later or those unfortunate men, like the father of this merchant, who never take it.

"Had our friend the merchant taken this step in his early manhood when this opportunity came to him, this day he would be blessed with much more of this world's goods. Should the good luck of our friend, the cloth weaver, cause him to take such a step at this time, it will indeed be but the beginning of much greater good fortune."

"Thank you. I'd like to speak also." A stranger from another country arose. "I am a Syrian. Not so well do I speak your tongue. I wish to call this friend, the merchant, a name. Maybe you think it not polite, this name. Yet I wish to call him that, but alas, I not know your word for it. If I do call it in Syrian, you will not understand. Therefore, please some good gentlemen, tell me that right name you call man who puts off doing those things that might be good for him."

"Procrastinator," called a voice.

"That's him," shouted the Syrian, waving his hands excitedly. "He accepts not opportunity when she comes. He waits. He says, 'I have much business right now. By and by I talk to you.' Opportunity, she will not wait for such slow fellow. She thinks if a man desires to be lucky, he will step quick. Any man not step quick when opportunity comes, he big procrastinator like our friend, this merchant."

The merchant arose and bowed good-naturedly in response to the laughter. "My admiration to thee, stranger within our gates, who hesitates not to speak the truth."

"And now let us hear another tale of opportunity. Who has for us another experience?" demanded Arkad.

"I have," responded a red-robed man of middle age. "I am a buyer of animals, mostly camels and horses. Sometimes I do also buy the sheep and goats. The tale I am about to relate will tell truthfully how opportunity came one night when I did least expect it. Perhaps for this reason I did let it escape. Of this, you shall be the judge.

"Returning to the city one evening after a disheartening ten days' journey in search of camels, I was much angered to find the gates of the city closed and locked. While my slaves spread our tent for the night, which we looked to spend with little food and no water, I was approached by an elderly farmer who, like ourselves, found himself locked outside.

"'Honored sir,' he addressed me, 'from thy appearance, I do judge thee to be a buyer. If this be so, much would I like to sell to thee the most excellent flock of sheep just driven up. Alas, my good wife lies very sick with the fever. I must return with all haste. Buy thou my sheep that I and my slaves may mount our camels and travel back without delay.'

"So dark it was that I could not see his flock, but from the bleating I did know it must be large. Having wasted ten days searching for camels I could not find, I was glad to bargain with him. In his anxiety, he did set a most reasonable price. I accepted, well knowing my slaves could drive the flock through the city gates in the morning and sell at a substantial profit.

"The bargain concluded. I called my slaves to bring torches, that we might count the flock, which the farmer declared to contain 900. I shall not burden you, my friends, with a description of our difficulty in attempting to count so many thirsty, restless, milling sheep. It proved to be an impossible task. Therefore I bluntly informed the farmer I would count them at daylight and pay him then.

"'Please, most honorable sir,' he pleaded, 'pay me but two-thirds of the price tonight, that I may be on my way. I will leave my most intelligent and educated slave to assist to make the count in the morning. He is trustworthy, and to him thou canst pay the balance.'

"But I was stubborn and refused to make payment that night. Next morning, before I awoke, the city gates opened, and four buyers rushed out in search of flocks. They were most eager and willing to pay high prices, because the city was threatened with siege and food was not plentiful. Nearly three times the price at which he had offered the flock to me did the old farmer receive for it. Thus was rare good luck allowed to escape."

"Here is a tale most unusual," commented Arkad. "What wisdom doth it suggest?"

"The wisdom of making a payment immediately when we are convinced our bargain is wise," suggested a venerable saddlemaker. "If the bargain be good, then dost thou need protection against thine own weaknesses as much as against any other man. We mortals are changeable. Alas, I must say more apt to change our minds when right than wrong. Wrong, we are stubborn indeed. Right, we are prone to vacillate and let opportunity escape. My first judgment is my best. Yet always have I found it difficult to compel myself to proceed with a good bargain when made. Therefore, as a protection against my own weaknesses, I do make a prompt deposit thereon. This doth save me from later regrets for the good luck that should have been mine."

"Thank you. Again, I'd like to speak." The Syrian was upon his feet once more. "These tales much alike. Each time opportunity fly away for same reason. Each time she come to procrastinator, bringing good plan. Each time they hesitate, not say, right now best time, I do it quick. How can men succeed that way?"

"Wise are thy words, my friend," responded the buyer. "Good luck fled from procrastination in both these tales. Yet this is not unusual. The spirit of procrastination is within all men. We desire riches, yet how often when opportunity doth appear before us, that spirit of procrastination from within doth urge various delays in our acceptance. In listening to it, we do become our own worst enemies.

"In my younger days I did not know it by this long word our friend from Syria doth enjoy. I did think at first it was my own poor judgment that did cause me loss of many profitable trades. Later I did credit it to my stubborn disposition. At last I did recognize it for what it was—a habit of needless delaying where action was required, action prompt and decisive. How I did hate it when its true character stood revealed. With the bitterness of a wild ass hitched to a chariot, I did break loose from this enemy to my success."

"Thank you. I'd like ask question from Mr. Merchant." The Syrian was speaking. "You wear fine robes, not like those of poor man. You speak like successful man. Tell us, do you listen now when procrastination whispers in your ear?"

"Like our friend the buyer, I also had to recognize and conquer procrastination," responded the merchant. "To me, it proved to be an enemy, ever watching and waiting to thwart my accomplishments. The tale I did relate is but one of many similar instances I could tell to show how it drove away my opportunities.

"'Tis not difficult to conquer, once understood. No man willingly permits the thief to rob his bins of grain. Nor does any man willingly permit an enemy to drive away his customers and rob him of his profits. When once I did recognize that such acts as these my enemy was committing, with determination I conquered him. So must every man master his own spirit of procrastination before he can expect to share in the rich treasures of Babylon.

"What sayest, Arkad? Because thou art the richest man in Babylon, many do proclaim thee to be the luckiest. Dost agree with me that no man can arrive at a full measure of success until he hath completely crushed the spirit of procrastination within him?"

"It is even as thou sayest," Arkad admitted. "During my long life I have watched generation following generation, marching forward along those avenues of trade, science, and learning that lead to success in life. Opportunities came to all these men. Some grasped theirs and moved steadily to the gratification of their deepest desires, but the majority hesitated, faltered, and fell behind."

Arkad turned to the cloth weaver. "Thou didst suggest that we debate good luck. Let us hear what thou now thinkest upon the subject."

"I do see good luck in a different light. I had thought of it as something most desirable that might happen to a man without effort upon his part. Now I do realize such happenings are not the sort of thing one may attract to himself. From our discussion have I learned to attract good luck to oneself, it is necessary to take advantage of opportunities. Therefore, in the future, I shall endeavor to make the best of such opportunities as do come to me."

"Thou hast well grasped the truths brought forth in our discussion," Arkad replied. "Good luck, we do find, often follows opportunity but seldom comes otherwise. Our merchant friend would have found great good luck had he accepted the opportunity the good goddess did present to him. Our friend the buyer likewise would have enjoyed good luck had he completed the purchase of the flock and sold at such a handsome profit.

"We did pursue this discussion to find a means by which good luck could be enticed to us. I feel that we have found the way. Both the tales did illustrate how good luck follows opportunity. Herein lies a truth that many similar tales of good luck, won or lost, could not change. The truth is this: good luck can be enticed by accepting opportunity.

"Those eager to grasp opportunities for their betterment do attract the interest of the good goddess. She is ever anxious to aid those who please her. Men of action please her best.

"Action will lead thee forward to the successes thou dost desire. Men of action are favored by the Goddess of Good Luck."

---

# ❧ Dan ☙

Do you believe in luck? We all know people who seem to be born lucky. Nothing bad ever seems to happen to them. They have a terrible car accident and then receive a huge insurance settlement. They get fired, but land a better job the next day. Is it just random luck? Are you a lucky person, or can you get some of that luck to rub off on you?

According to Brian Tracy in his program "The Luck Factor," luck isn't a random whim of fate. It's not something that happens by chance. No, luck is predictable. You can actually control luck. The keys that Brian Tracy talks about are the very ones in *The Richest Man in Babylon*.

Arkad said that the way to attract good luck is to take advantage of opportunities when they come along, because the Goddess of Good Luck can be enticed by accepting opportunities. Those who are eager to grasp opportunities for their betterment do attract the interest of the Goddess of Good Luck. The ones who please the goddess are men of action.

As Brian Tracy puts it, "Luck is a matter of probabilities." There's a certain probability that anything can happen, and these probabilities can be calculated with considerable accuracy. Therefore luck is a function of activity. The more things you try and the faster you try them, the more likely you are to try the right thing at the right time, which will bring you the success that you desire.

It's like the homely man who asks every single girl he meets out on a date. The more girls he asks out, the higher the probability is that one of them will say yes. Sure, he'll get rejected more, but he's also more likely to achieve his goal. The fact is, most of the things you try don't work the first time. Often they don't work the first ten times. Nonetheless, if you keep trying new things and learning from every setback, you'll inevitably attract the attention of the Goddess of Good Luck.

What are some things that you can do to attract good luck? One thing is, you have to continually study and prepare. Motivation speaker Earl Nightingale said that if a person doesn't prepare for his success, when the opportunity comes, it will only make him look foolish.

You've probably heard it said that luck is what happens when preparedness meets opportunity. Only when you've paid the price of being ready for your success will you be in a position to take advantage of opportunities when they arise.

The most remarkable thing is this: the very act of preparation attracts to you, like iron filings to a magnet, opportunities to use that preparation to advance your life. In preparing for success, one of the best questions that you can ask yourself continually is this: what can I do that, if done well, will make a difference in my career?

Take some time now to get your journal and answer this question: what can I do that, if done well, will make a difference in my career?

Another way to prepare yourself for success is to read. Self-publishing guru Dan Poynter gives us some shocking statistics. Did you know that one-third of high school graduates never read another book for the rest of their lives? That 42 percent of college graduates never read another book after college? That 80 percent of U.S. families did not buy or read a book last year? That 70 percent of U.S. adults have not been in a bookstore in the last five years? Or that 57 percent of new books are not read to completion?

This is shocking and saddening. Research has shown that people who start the day by reading for a half an hour before doing anything else are more successful than those who check emails and return phone calls. So your action step is pretty obvious. Get a book, and start reading it.

But you might say, "Dan, I don't like reading." Have you tried recently?

Maybe you used to dislike reading, but it's because you weren't interested in the subject matter. Go ahead and go to the library and check out a book on a subject that interests you. It doesn't even have to be business or wealth-related. Just get in the habit of reading every morning, and you'll start attracting opportunities to you like iron filings to a magnet.

Let's talk for a minute about goal setting. Luck seems to happen to people with clear goals and detailed plans of action. As Arkad said, luck favors men and women of action. How clear are your goals? Do you have them written down?

Having clear goals in every area of your life is important. In your journal, make a list of specific goals for every major area of your life. Choose goals in the areas of health, relationships, spiritual growth, work or career, and of course, finance. Then, next to the goal, write down one action you're committed to taking in the next twenty-four hours or so. When you know exactly what you want and are working diligently to achieve it every day, all kinds of wonderful things happen to you to move you more rapidly towards your goals and bring them towards you.

## Babylon Builder

In this chapter, we learned that luck is not accidental. It's a function of taking action and being prepared for opportunity. We also talked about the importance of having clear goals and identifying what actions you can take.

So for your action steps, you identified things you can do to become more lucky. You listed some actions you can take to become prepared for opportunity. You made a commitment to start reading every morning. Then you made a list of goals for each of the major areas of your life and identified at least one action step you can take to reach each goal. Hopefully, you've even taken those steps.

# SIX
# The Five Laws
# of Gold

A bag heavy with gold or a clay tablet carved with words of wisdom; if thou hadst thy choice, which wouldst thou choose?" By the flickering light from the fire of desert shrubs, the suntanned faces of the listeners gleamed with interest.

"The gold, the gold," chorused the twenty-seven.

Old Kalabab smiled knowingly. "Hark," he resumed, raising his hand. "Hear the wild dogs out there in the night. They howl and wail because they are lean with hunger. Yet feed them, and what do they? Fight and strut. Then fight and strut some more, giving no thought to the morrow that will surely come.

"Just so it is with the sons of men. Give them a choice of gold and wisdom, what do they do? Ignore the wisdom and waste the gold. On the morrow they wail because they have no more gold.

"Gold is reserved for those who know its laws and abide by them."

Kalabab drew his white robe close about his lean legs, for a cool night wind was blowing. "Because thou hast served me faithfully upon our long journey, because thou caredst well for my camels, because thou toiledst uncomplainingly across the hot sands of the desert, because thou fought bravely the robbers that sought to despoil my merchandise, I will tell thee this night the tale of the Five Laws of Gold, such a tale as thou never hast heard before. Hark ye, with deep attention to the words I speak, for if you grasp their meaning and heed them, in the days that come thou shalt have much gold."

He paused impressively. Above in a canopy of blue, the stars shone brightly in the crystal-clear skies of Babylonia. Behind the group loomed their faded tents tightly staked against possible desert storms. Beside the tents were neatly stacked bales of merchandise covered with skins. Nearby the camel herd sprawled in the sand, some chewing their cuds contentedly, others snoring in hoarse discord.

"Thou hast told us many good tales, Kalabab," spoke up the chief packer. "We look to thy wisdom to guide us upon the morrow when our service with thee shall be at an end."

"I have but told thee of my adventures in strange and distant lands, but this night I shall tell thee of the wisdom of Arkad, the wise rich man."

"Much have we heard of him," acknowledged the chief packer, "for he was the richest man that ever lived in Babylon."

"The richest man he was, and that because be was wise in the ways of gold, even as no man had ever been before him. This night shall I tell you of his great wisdom as it was told to me by Nomasir, his son, many years ago in Nineveh, when I was but a lad.

"My master and myself had tarried long into the night in the palace of Nomasir. I had helped my master bring great bundles of fine rugs, each one to be tried by Nomasir until his choice of colors was satisfied. At last he was well pleased and commanded us to sit with him and to drink a rare vintage odorous to the nostrils and most warming to my stomach, which was unaccustomed to such a drink.

"Then did he tell us this tale of the great wisdom of Arkad, his father, even as I shall tell it to you.

"In Babylon it is the custom, as you know, that the sons of wealthy fathers live with their parents in expectation of inheriting the estate. Arkad did not approve of this custom. Therefore, when Nomasir reached man's estate, he sent for the young man and addressed him.

"'My son, it is my desire that thou succeed to my estate. Thou must, however, first prove that thou art capable of wisely handling it. Therefore, I wish that thou go out into the world and show thine ability both to acquire gold and to make thyself-respected among men. To start thee well, I will give thee two things of which I myself was denied when I started as a poor youth to build up a fortune. First, I give thee this bag of gold. If thou use it wisely, it will be the basis of thy future success.

"'Second, I give thee this clay tablet upon which is carved the Five Laws of Gold. If thou dost but interpret them in thine own acts, they shall bring thee competence and security.

"'Ten years from this day come thou back to the house of thy father and give account of thyself. If thou prove worthy, I will then make thee the heir to my estate. Otherwise I will give it to the priests, that they may barter for my soul the kind consideration of the gods.'

"So Nomasir went forth to make his own way, taking his bag of gold, the clay tablet carefully wrapped in silken cloth, his slave, and the horses upon which they rode.

"The ten years passed, and Nomasir, as he had agreed, returned to the house of his father, who provided a great feast in his honor, to which he invited many friends and relatives. After the feast was over, the father and mother mounted their thronelike seats at one side of the great hall, and Nomasir stood before them to give an account of himself, as he had promised his father.

"It was evening. The room was hazy with smoke from the wicks of the oil lamps that but dimly lighted it. Slaves in white woven jackets and tunics fanned the humid air rhythmically with long-stemmed palm leaves. A stately dignity colored the scene. The wife of Nomasir and his two young sons, with friends and other members of the family, sat upon rugs behind him, eager listeners.

"'My father,' he began deferentially, 'I bow before thy wisdom. Ten years ago, when I stood at the gates of manhood, thou badest me go forth and become a man among men, instead of remaining a vassal to thy fortune. Thou gavest me liberally of thy gold. Thou gave me liberally of thy wisdom. Of the gold, alas, I must admit of a disastrous handling. It fled, indeed, from my inexperienced hands even as a wild hare flees at the first opportunity from the youth who captures it.'

"The father smiled indulgently. 'Continue, my son, thy tale interests me in all its details.'

"'I decided to go to Nineveh, as it was a growing city, believing that I might find there opportunities. I joined a caravan and among its members made numerous friends. Two well-spoken men who had a most beautiful white horse as fleet as the wind were among these.

"As we journeyed, they told me in confidence that in Nineveh was a wealthy man who owned a horse so swift that it had never been beaten. Its owner believed that no horse living could run with greater speed. Therefore, would he wager any sum, however large, that his horse could outspeed any horse in all Babylonia? Compared to their horse, so my friends said, it was but a lumbering ass that could be beaten with ease.

"'They offered, as a great favor, to permit me to join them in a wager. I was quite carried away with the plan.

"'Our horse was badly beaten, and I lost much of my gold.' The father laughed.

"'Later I discovered that this was a deceitful plan of these men, and they constantly journeyed with cara-vans, seeking victims. You see, the man in Nineveh was their partner and shared with them the bets he won. This shrewd deceit taught me my first lesson in looking out for myself.

"'I was soon to learn another, equally bitter. In the caravan was another young man, with whom I became quite friendly. He was the son of wealthy parents and, like myself, journeying to Nineveh to find a suitable location. Not long after our arrival, he told me that a merchant had died, and his shop with its rich merchandise and patronage could be secured at a paltry price. Saying that we would be equal partners, but first he must return to Babylon to secure his gold, he prevailed upon me to purchase the stock with my gold, agreeing that his would be used later to carry on our venture.

"'He long delayed the trip to Babylon, proving in the meantime to be an unwise buyer and a foolish spender. I finally put him out, but not before the business had deteriorated to where we had only unsalable goods and no gold to buy other goods. I sacrificed what was left to an Israelite for a pitiful sum.

"'Soon there followed, I tell you, my father, bitter days. I sought employment and found it not, for I was without trade or training that would enable me to earn. I sold my horses. I sold my slave. I sold my extra robes that I might have food and a place to sleep, but each day grim want crouched closer.

"'But in those bitter days, I remembered thy confidence in me, my father. Thou hadst sent me forth to become a man, and this I was determined to accomplish.'

"The mother buried her face and wept softly.

"'At this time, I bethought me of the table thou hadst given to me upon which thou had carved the Five Laws of

Gold. Thereupon, I read most carefully thy words of wisdom, and realized that had I but sought wisdom first, my gold would not have been lost to me. I learned by heart each law and determined that, when once more the goddess of good fortune smiled upon me, I would be guided by the wisdom of age and not by the inexperience of youth.

"'For the benefit of you who are seated here this night, I will read the wisdom of my father as engraved upon the clay tablet which he gave to me ten years ago.

"'The Five Laws of Gold. One, gold cometh gladly and in increasing quantity to any man who will put by not less than one-tenth of his earnings to create an estate for his future and that of his family.

"'Two, gold laboreth diligently and contentedly for the wise owner who finds for it profitable employment, multiplying even as the flocks of the field.

"'Three, gold clingeth to the protection of the cautious owner who invests it under the advice of men wise in its handling.

"'Four, gold slippeth away from the man who invests it in businesses or purposes with which he is not familiar or which are not approved by those skilled in its keep.

"'Five, gold flees the man who would force it to impossible earnings or who followeth the alluring advice of tricksters and schemers or who trusts it to his own inexperience and romantic desires in investment.

"'These are the Five Laws of Gold as written by my father. I do proclaim them as of greater value than gold itself, as I will show by the continuance of my tale.'

"He again faced his father. 'I have told thee of the depth of poverty and despair to which my inexperience brought me. However, there is no chain of disasters that will not come to an end. Mine came when I secured employment managing a crew of slaves working upon the new outer wall of the city.

"'Profiting from my knowledge of the first law of gold, I saved a copper from my first earnings, adding to it at every opportunity until I had a piece of silver. It was a slow procedure, for one must live. I did spend grudgingly, I admit, because I was determined to earn back before the ten years were over as much gold as you, my father, had given to me.

"'One day the slave master, with whom I had become quite friendly, said to me, "Thou art a thrifty youth who spends not wantonly what he earns. Hast thou gold put by that is not earning?"

"'Yes,' I replied. 'It is my greatest desire to accumulate gold to replace that which my father gave to me and which I have lost.'

""'Tis a worthy ambition, I will grant, and do you know that the gold which you have saved can work for you and earn much more gold?'"

"'Alas, my experience has been bitter, for my father's gold has fled from me, and I am in much fear lest my own do the same.'

""'If thou hast confidence in me, I will give thee a lesson in the profitable handling of gold," he replied. "Within a year the outer wall will be complete and ready for the great gates of bronze that will be built at each entrance to protect the city from the king's enemies. In all Nineveh there is not enough metal to make these gates, and the king has not thought to provide it.

""Here is my plan. A group of us will pool our gold and send a caravan to the mines of copper and tin, which are distant, and bring to Nineveh the metal for the gates. When the king says, 'Make the great gates,' we alone can supply the metal, and a rich price he will pay. If the king will not buy from us, we will yet have the metal which can be sold for a fair price.'"

"'In his offer I recognized an opportunity to abide by the third law and invest my savings under the guidance of wise men. Nor was I disappointed. Our pool was a success, and my small store of gold was greatly increased by the transaction.

"'In due time, I was accepted as a member of this same group in other ventures. They were men wise in the profitable handling of gold. They talked over each plan presented with great care before entering upon it. They would take no chance on losing their principal or tying it up in unprofitable investments from which their gold could not be recovered. Such foolish things as the horse race and the partnership into which I had entered with my inexperience would have had scant consideration with them. They would have immediately pointed out their weaknesses.

"'Through my association with these men, I learned to safely invest gold to bring profitable returns. As the years went on, my treasure increased more and more rapidly. I not only made back as much as I lost, but much more.

Through my misfortunes, my trials and my success, I have tested time and again the wisdom of the Five Laws of Gold, my father, and have proven them true in every test. To him who is without knowledge of the five laws, gold comes not often, and goeth away quickly, but to him who abide by the five laws, gold comes and works as his dutiful slave.'

"Nomasir ceased speaking and motioned to a slave in the back of the room. The slave brought forward, one at a time, three heavy leather bags. One of these Nomasir took and placed upon the floor before his father, addressing him again. 'Thou didst give to me a bag of gold, Babylon gold. Behold in its place, I do return to thee a bag of Nineveh gold of equal weight, an equal exchange, as all will agree.

"'Thou didst give to me a clay tablet inscribed with wisdom. Behold, in its stead, I do return two bags of gold.' So saying, he took from the slave the other two bags and, likewise, placed them upon the floor before his father. 'This I do to prove to thee, my father, of how much greater value I consider thy wisdom than thy gold. Yet who can measure in bags of gold the value of wisdom? Without wisdom, gold is quickly lost by those who have it, but with wisdom, gold can be secured by those who have it not, as these three bags of gold do prove.

"'It does indeed give to me the deepest satisfaction, my father, to stand before thee and say that, because of thy wisdom, I have been able to become rich and respected before men.'

"The father placed his hand fondly upon the head of Nomasir. 'Thou hast learned well thy lessons, and I am indeed fortunate to have a son to whom I may entrust my wealth.'"

Kalabab ceased his tale and looked critically at his listeners. "What means this to thee, this tale of Nomasir?" he continued. "Who amongst thee can go to thy father or to the father of thy wife and give an account of wise handling of his earnings? What would these venerable men think were you to say, 'I have traveled much and learned much and labored much and earned much, yet alas, of gold I have little. Some I spent wisely, some I spent foolishly, and much I lost in unwise ways.'

"Dost still think it but an inconsistency of fate that some men have much gold and others have naught? Then you err.

"Men have much gold when they know the Five Laws of Gold and abide thereby.

"Because I learned these five laws in my youth and abided by them, I have become a wealthy merchant. Not by some strange magic did I accumulate my wealth.

"Wealth that comes quickly goeth the same way.

"Wealth that stayeth to give enjoyment and satisfaction to its owner comes gradually, because it is a child born of knowledge and persistent purpose.

"To earn wealth is but a slight burden upon the thoughtful man. Bearing the burden consistently from year to year accomplishes the final purpose.

"The Five Laws of Gold offer to thee a rich reward for their observance. Each of these five laws is rich with meaning, and lest thou overlook this in the briefness of my tale, I will now repeat them. I do know them each by heart, because in my youth, I could see their value and would not be content until I knew them word for word.

"The First Law of Gold: *Gold cometh gladly and in increasing quantity to any man who will put by not less than one-tenth of his earnings to create an estate for his future and that of his family.* Any man who will put by one-tenth of his earnings consistently and invest it wisely will surely create a valuable estate that will provide an income for him in the future and further guarantee safety for his family in case the gods call him to the world of darkness.

"This law always sayeth that gold cometh gladly to such a man. I can truly certify this in my own life. The more gold I accumulate, the more readily it comes to me and in increased quantities. The gold which I save earns more, even as yours will, and its earnings earn more, and this is the working out of the first law.

"The Second Law of Gold: *Gold laboreth diligently and contentedly for the wise owner who finds for it profitable employment, multiplying even as the flocks of the field.*

"Gold, indeed, is a willing worker. It is ever eager to multiply when opportunity presents itself. To every man who hath a store of gold set by, opportunity comes for its most profitable use. As the years pass, it multiplies itself in surprising fashion.

"The Third Law of Gold: *Gold clingeth to the protection of the cautious owner who invests it under the advice of men wise in its handling.* Gold indeed clingeth to the cautious owner, even as it flees the careless owner. The man who seeks the advice of men wise in handling gold soon learneth not to jeopardize his treasure, but to preserve in safety and to enjoy in contentment its consistent increase.

"The Fourth Law of Gold: *Gold slippeth away from the man who invests it in businesses or purposes with which he is not familiar or which are not approved by those skilled in its keep.* To the man who hath gold, yet is not skilled in its handling, many uses for it appear most profitable. Too often these are fraught with danger of loss, and if properly analyzed by wise men, show small possibility of profit.

"Therefore the inexperienced owner of gold who trusts to his own judgment and invests it in businesses or purposes with which he is not familiar too often finds his judgment imperfect, and pays with his treasure for his inexperience. Wise indeed is he who investeth his treasures under the advice of men skilled in the ways of gold.

"The Fifth Law of Gold: *Gold flees the man who would force it to impossible earnings or who followeth the alluring advice of tricksters and schemers or who trusts it to his own inexperience and romantic desires in investment.*

"Fanciful propositions that thrill like adventure tales always come to the new owner of gold. These appear to endow his treasure with magic powers that will enable it to make impossible earnings. Yet heed he the wise men, for verily they know the risks that lurk behind every plan to make great wealth suddenly. Forget not the rich men of Nineveh, who would take no chance of losing their principal or tying it up in unprofitable investments.

"This ends my tale of the Five Laws of Gold. In telling it to thee, I have told the secrets of my own success. Yet they are not secrets but truths, which every man must first learn and then follow who wishes to step out of the multitude that, like yon wild dogs, must worry each day for food to eat.

"Tomorrow we enter Babylon. Look! see the fire that burns eternal above the Temple of Bel. We are already in sight of the golden city.

"Tomorrow each of thee shall have gold, the gold thou has so well earned by thy faithful services.

"Ten years from this night, what can you tell about this gold? If there be men among you, who, like Nomasir, will use a portion of their gold to start for themselves an estate and be thenceforth wisely guided by the wisdom of Arkad, ten years from now, 'tis a safe wager, like the son of Arkad, they will be rich and respected among men.

"Our wise acts accompany us through life to please us and to help us. Just as surely, our unwise acts follow us to plague and torment us. Alas, they cannot be forgotten. In the front rank of the torments that do follow us are the memories of the things we should have done, of the opportunities which came to us and we took not.

"Rich are the treasures of Babylon, so rich no man can count their value in pieces of gold. Each year, they grow richer and more valuable. Like the treasures of every land, they are a reward, a rich reward awaiting those men of purpose who determine to secure their just share.

"In the strength of thine own desires is a magic power. Guide this power with thy knowledge of the Five Laws of Gold and thou shall share the treasures of Babylon."

# ⤳ Dan ⤶

The Five Laws of Gold are basically a recap of the things we've learned so far. Law number one: "Gold cometh gladly and in increasing quantity to any man who will put by not less than one-tenth of his earnings to create an estate for his future and that of his family."

How are you doing with this? Have you started to save 10 percent of your income? Money will be attracted to you if you show it that you value it enough to save it.

Law number two: "Gold laboreth diligently and contentedly for the wise owner who finds for it profitable employment, multiplying even as the flocks of the field." This is saying that money wants to work for you. Invest your money, make it work for you, and it will multiply. Have you put your money to work for you?

Law number three: "Gold clingeth to the protection of the cautious owner who invests it under the advice of men wise in its handling." Have you met with a financial advisor yet? Money will cling to you if you're cautious and invest it under the advice of wise men or women.

Law number four: "Gold slippeth away from the man who invests it in businesses or purposes with which he is not familiar or which are not approved by those skilled in its keep." We've all done this before. Money will slip away from a person who tries to invest it in something that seems too good to be true or in a business that he or she knows nothing about. If you're a personal trainer, it's probably not a good idea to open an Italian restaurant without consulting someone who knows a lot about how to run a restaurant.

Law number five: "Gold flees the man who would force it to impossible earning, or who followeth the alluring advice of tricksters and schemers or who trust it to his own inexperience and romantic desires in investment." Money will run away from you if you try to force it into impossible situations or take the advice of tricksters.

Money is like a golden retriever. It wants to be with you, wants to work for you, will sit close by you if you show it that you can protect it, but it will run away if you abuse or neglect it.

Let's talk about some more ways to follow the Five Laws of Gold in modern times. To start, let's talk about paying yourself first. As David Bach says in *The Automatic Millionaire*, there's only one way to legally pay yourself first—meaning before taxes—and that's to put some pretax money into a retirement account. This means a 401(k), IRA, Keogh account, or similar vehicle. If you set this up through your employer, the money will be deducted automatically, and voilà, you're paying yourself first.

In an article for The Motley Fool website, author Chuck Saletta says that there are certain universal truths about investing for your retirement, and they hold up no matter how the market behaves. To be successful, you need to build and execute your retirement plan around (1) how much you currently have saved and can add to your savings each month; (2) what long-run rate of your return rate you're aiming to receive; (3) how much money you need to live each year and how bad inflation will be; and (4) when you plan to retire and how long you expect to live.

We've already addressed a few of these. In our Latte Factor exercise, we found money for you to sock away for savings. We've taken a look at how much money you'll need to retire and when that might be. So, really, the only one not covered is the rate of return you're aiming to receive. This is largely a matter of personality.

Some people are so scared of the stock market that they invest in conservative CDs that pay only 1 percent interest. Others look at stock declines as a huge sale and buy more stocks than ever. As Chuck Saletta put it:

Before completely turning away from the stock market, remember that those stocks are more than just pieces of paper. They represent ownership stakes in companies that are often very profitable. When you buy their shares, either directly or through a mutual fund, you buy a slice of their business and their future profit stream.

While the stock market may gyrate in the near term, over the long haul your shares will more or less mirror the value of the underlying business. In the short term, a market panic can take everyone's retirement savings for a roller-coaster ride. Over time, the panic will subside, and the strongest companies and their stocks will once again thrive. If you take this opportunity to reassess and retool your plans based on that current reality, you very likely can still position yourself to reach a successful retirement.

Let's talk a bit more about laws 3, 4, and 5—investing money. If you're thinking about investing your money in something, you need to understand the difference between an *asset* and a *liability.*

An asset is something you own. There are two kinds of assets: *liquid assets* and *investment assets.* Liquid assets are financial assets that are held in the form of cash or in instruments that can be readily converted to cash with little or no loss of value.

In other words, *liquid* means you can get your hands on the money relatively quickly and easily. Cash in your wallet, a bank account, a money-market account, a money-market mutual fund, and a certificate of deposit with less than a year to maturity would all be considered liquid assets. Liquid assets are available if needed to pay for current expenses. This is what the 90 percent of your income should be used for.

*Investment assets,* as the term implies, are securities you own for the purpose of earning a return rather than for spending on current living expenses or consumer purchases. This is the 10 percent that should be used to make your money work for you. Investments can include paper or intangible assets like stocks, bonds, and mutual-fund shares. They can also include business ownership, investment real estate, the cash value in a life-insurance policy or pension, retirement accounts like IRAs and 401(k) plans, commodities, financial futures, and options.

Here's your first exercise for this chapter. In your journal, make a list of all your assets. Remember to only list true assets—things you really own. Try to get an estimate of what they're worth. List them all and add up their value.

Now let's move to the other side of the balance sheet and look at your liabilities. Liabilities are an individual's or a household's debts. These are amounts of money you owe anyone for any reason—money you'll have to pay back in the future—and it doesn't matter if interest is being charged or not.

This is where many people get it wrong. They believe that simply increasing their assets is making them wealthier, so they use debt to buy an asset. It doesn't work this way. If you owe more money than you have in assets, you're not wealthy. This is another reason why you want to pay your home mortgage off as quickly as possible. It's not an asset until it's paid off. Until then, it's a great big liability.

Now you probably know what the next exercise is, don't you? Make a list of all your liabilities. This is all the money you owe, from your student loans to your mortgage to the money you owe your sister for that vacation to Cancún. Make the list, and add up the amounts. Oh, and get some tissues for yourself if you get depressed.

Now you have a list of your assets and a list of your liabilities. Take a look at them, and subtract your liabilities from your assets. This is what is called your *net worth*. Don't get too depressed if the number is small or even if it's negative. That's why you're here. You are here to learn how to change it and build real wealth.

I want to remind you why this is important. Remember back in chapter 1, when Bansir was musing that he'd probably always be poor? In the audio program "The Wealth Generator," John Cummuta brings it home in a powerful way:

> Let's be honest here. Building real wealth, the kind you can retire and live comfortably on, is not some marginally important, low-impact activity. It's crucially important, because there will come a day when you won't want to work as much or maybe at all, and you'll only have the option to throttle it back if you've built enough wealth to support you whether or not you're bringing in a current paycheck at the time. It won't just happen automatically. It won't just somehow all work out.

Your exercise is to look around you as you go through your day today and to note all the people you see who are obviously beyond retirement age but who are handing you coffee in a restaurant or a shopping cart at your favorite discount store. Do you think they planned to be standing eight hours a day and getting paid low wages at this point in their lives, or did they simply not plan at all and end up there by default?

I'm sure there are some people in these circumstances who are there through no fault of their own, who are victims of bad luck or an illness in the family that drained away their assets. But I know for a fact that most of them are there because they failed to plan to be in a better position in their so-called golden years. Failing to plan is planning to fail. It's the result of naively being lulled into complacency by circumstances that appear to be OK for right now.

This is why the lessons you're learning here are so vitally important in modern society. By following the Five Laws of Gold, you can prevent your future from being bleak and instead create the wealth you deserve.

### Babylon Builder

In this chapter, we learned about the Five Laws of Gold. We also learned some specific techniques for saving 10 percent of your dollars. We learned how to regroup if your retirement account has taken a hit. We also learned the difference between an asset and a liability, and we learned why planning for your retirement is important so that you don't end up working under the golden arches in your golden years.

For action steps, you listed your assets and your liabilities and determined your net worth. Maybe you had a little cry when you saw that number, but then you realized how important it is to start planning now for retirement. You also observed that a lot of people who didn't plan well enough, and hopefully that motivated you to keep taking the actions you're taking in this program.

Now let's move onto the next chapter, where we'll learn all about borrowing and lending money.

# SEVEN
# The Gold Lender
# of Babylon ·

Fifty pieces of gold. Never before had Rodan, the spear-maker of old Babylon, carried so much gold in his leather wallet. Happily down the king's highway from the palace of his most liberal Majesty he strode. Cheerfully the gold clinked as the wallet at his belt swayed with each step, the sweetest music he had ever heard.

Fifty pieces of gold, all his. He could hardly realize his good fortune. What power in those clinking discs! They could purchase anything he wanted, a grand house, land, cattle, camels, horses, chariots, whatever he might desire.

What use should he make of it? This evening, as he turned into a side street towards the home of his sister, he could think of nothing he would rather possess than those same glittering, heavy pieces of gold, his to keep.

It was upon an evening some days later that a per-plexed Rodan entered the shop of Mathon, the lender of gold and dealer in jewels and rare fabrics. Glancing neither to the right nor the left at the colorful articles artfully displayed, he passed through to the living quarters at the rear. Here he found the genteel Mathon lounging upon a rug, partaking of a meal served by a black slave.

"I would counsel with thee, for I know not what to do." Rodan stood stolidly, feet apart, hairy breast exposed by the gaping front of his leather jacket. Mathon's narrow, sallow face smiled a friendly greeting.

"What indiscretions hast thou done that thou shouldst seek the lender of gold? Hast been unlucky at the gaming table? Or hath some plump dame entangled thee? For many years have I known thee, yet never hast thou sought me to aid thee in thy troubles."

"No, no. Not such as that. I seek no gold. Instead I crave thy wise advice."

"Hear, hear what this man doth say! No one comes to the lender of gold for advice. My ears must play me false."

"They listen true."

"Can this be so? Rodan the spearmaker doth display more cunning than all the rest, for he comes to Mathon, not for gold, but for advice. Many men come to me for gold to pay for their follies, but as for advice, they want it not. Yet who is more able to advise than the lender of gold to whom many men come in trouble?

"Thou shalt eat with me, Rodan," he continued. "Thou shalt be my guest for the evening. Andol," he commanded of the black slave, "draw up a rag for my friend, Rodan, the spearmaker, who comes for advice. He shall be mine honored guest. Bring to him much food and get for him my largest cup. Choose well of the best wine, that he may have satisfaction in the drinking. Now tell me what troubles thee."

"It is the king's gift."

"The king's gift? The king did make thee a gift and it gives thee trouble? What manner of gift?"

"Because he was much pleased with the design I did submit to him for a new point on the spears of the royal guard, he did present me with fifty pieces of gold, and now I am much perplexed. I am beseeched each hour the sun doth travel across the sky by those who would share it with me."

"That is natural. More men want gold than have it, and would wish one who comes by it easily to divide, but can you not say no? Is thy will not as strong as thy fist?"

"To many I can say no, yet sometimes it would be easier to say yes. Can one refuse to share with one's sister, to whom he is deeply devoted?"

"Surely thine own sister would not wish to deprive thee of enjoying thy reward."

"But, it is for the sake of Araman, her husband, whom she wishes to see a rich merchant. She does feel that he has never had a chance, and she beseeches me to loan to him this gold, that he may become a prosperous merchant and repay me from his profits."

"My friend," resumed Mathon, "'tis a worthy subject thou bringest to discuss. Gold bringeth unto its possessor responsibility and a changed position with his fellow men. It bringeth fear lest he lose it or it be tricked away from him. It bringeth a feeling of power and ability to do good.

Likewise it bringeth opportunities whereby his very good intentions may bring him into difficulties.

"Didst ever hear of the farmer of Nineveh who could understand the language of animals? I wot not, for 'tis not the kind of tale men like to tell over the bronze caster's forge. I will tell it to thee, for thou shouldst know that to borrowing and lending there is more than the passing of gold from the hands of one to the hands of another.

"This farmer, who could understand what the animals said to each other, did linger in the farmyard each evening just to listen to their words. One evening he did hear the ox bemoaning to the ass the hardness of his lot. 'I do labor pulling the plow from morning until night. No matter how hot the day, or how tired my legs, or how the bow doth chafe my neck, still must I work. But you are a creature of leisure. You are trapped with a colorful blanket and do nothing more than carry our master about where he wishes to go. When he goes nowhere, you do rest and eat the green grass all the day.'

"Now the ass, in spite of his vicious heels, was a goodly fellow and sympathized with the ox. 'My good friend,' he replied, 'you do work very hard, and I would help ease your lot. Therefore will I tell you how you may have a day of rest. In the morning when the slave comes to fetch you to the plow, lie upon the ground and bellow much, that he may say you are sick and cannot work.'

"So the ox took the advice of the ass, and the next morning the slave returned to the farmer and told him the ox was sick and could not pull the plow. 'Then,' said the farmer, 'hitch the ass to the plow, for the plowing must go on.'

"All that day the ass, who had only intended to help his friend, found himself compelled to do the ox's task. When night came and he was released from the plow, his heart was bitter and his legs were weary, and his neck was sore where the bow had chafed it. The farmer lingered in the barnyard to listen.

"The ox began first. 'You are my good friend. Because of your wise advice I have enjoyed a day of rest.'

"'And I,' retorted the ass, 'am like many another simple-hearted ones who starts to help a friend and ends up by doing his task for him. Hereafter you draw your own plow, for I did hear the master tell the slave to send for the butcher were you sick again. I wish he would, for you are a lazy fellow.'

"Thereafter they spoke to each other no more. This ended their friendship. Canst thou tell the moral to this tale, Rodan?"

"'Tis a good tale," responded Rodan, "but I see not the moral."

"I thought not that you would, but it is there, and simple too. Just this: if you desire to help thy friend, do so in a way that will not bring thy friend's burdens upon thyself."

"I had not thought of that. It is a wise moral. I wish not to assume the burdens of my sister's husband, but tell me. You lend to many. Do not the borrowers repay?"

Mathon smiled the smile of one whose soul is rich with much experience. "Could a loan be well made if the borrower cannot repay? Must not the lender be wise and judge carefully whether his gold can perform a useful purpose to the borrower and return to him once more, or whether it will be wasted by one unable to use it wisely and leave him without his treasure, and leave the borrower with a debt he cannot repay? I will show to thee the tokens in my token chest and let them tell thee some of their stories."

Into the room he brought a chest as long as his arm, covered with red pigskin and ornamented with bronze designs. He placed it upon the floor and squatted before it, both hands upon the lid.

"From each person to whom I lend, I do exact a token for my token chest, to remain there until the loan is repaid. When they repay I give back, but if they never repay, it will always remind me of one who was not faithful to my confidence.

"The safest loans, my token box tells me, are to those whose possessions are of more value than the one they desire. They own lands, or jewels, or camels, or other things which could be sold to repay the loan. Some of the tokens given to me are jewels of more value than the loan. Others are promises that if the loan be not repaid as agreed, they will deliver to me certain property settlement. On loans like those, I am assured that my gold will be returned with the rental thereon, for the loan is based on property.

"In another class are those who have the capacity to earn. They are such as you, who labor or serve and are paid. They have income, and if they are honest and suffer no misfortune, I know that they also can repay the gold I loan them and the rental to which I am entitled. Such loans are based on human effort.

"Others are those who have neither property nor assured earning capacity. Life is hard, and there will always be some who cannot adjust themselves to it. Alas for the loans I make them, even though they be no larger than a penny! My token box may censure me in the years to come unless they be guaranteed by good friends of the borrower who know him honorable."

Mathon released the clasp and opened the lid. Rodan leaned forward eagerly. At the top of the chest a bronze neckpiece lay upon a scarlet cloth. Mathon picked up the piece and patted it affectionately. "This shall always remain in my token chest because the owner has passed on into the great darkness. I treasure it, his token, and I treasure his memory, for he was my good friend. We traded together with much success until out of the east he brought a woman to wed, beautiful, but not like our women. A dazzling creature. He spent his gold lavishly to gratify her desires.

"He came to me in distress when his gold was gone. I counseled with him. I told him I would help him to once more master his own affairs. He swore by the sign of the Great Bull that he would, but it was not to be. In a quarrel she thrust a knife into the heart he dared her to pierce."

"And she?" questioned Rodan.

"Yes, of course, this was hers." He picked up the scarlet cloth. "In bitter remorse she threw herself into the Euphrates. These two loans will never be repaid. The chest tells you, Rodan, that humans in the throes of great emotions are not safe risks for the gold lender. Here, now this is different."

He reached for a ring carved of ox bone. "This belongs to a farmer. I buy the rugs of his women. The locusts came, and they had not food. I helped him, and when the new crop came he repaid me. Later, he came again and told of strange goats in a distant land as described by a traveler. They had long hair so fine and soft it would weave into rugs more beautiful than any ever seen in Babylon. He wanted a herd but he had no money.

"So I did lend him gold to make the journey and bring back goats. Now his herd is begun, and next year I shall surprise the lords of Babylon with the most expensive rugs it has been their good fortune to buy. Soon I must return his ring. He doth insist on repaying promptly."

"Some borrowers do that?" queried Rodan.

"If they borrow for purposes that bring money back to them, I find it so, but if they borrow because of their indiscretions, I warn thee to be cautious if thou wouldst ever have thy gold back in hand again."

"Tell me about this," requested Rodan, picking up a heavy gold bracelet inset with jewels in rare designs.

"The women do appeal to my good friend," bantered Mathon.

"I am still much younger than you," retorted Rodan.

"I grant that, but this time thou doth suspicion romance where it is not. The owner of this is fat and wrinkled and doth talk so much and say so little she drives me mad. Once they had much money and were good customers, but ill times came upon them. She has a son of whom she would make a merchant. So she came to me and borrowed gold, that he might become a partner of a caravan owner who travels with his camels, bartering in one city what he buys in another.

"This man proved a rascal, for he left the poor boy in a distant city without money and without friends, pulling out early while the youth slept. Perhaps when this youth has grown to manhood, he will repay; until then I get no rental for the loan, only much talk, but I do admit the jewels are worthy of the loan."

"Did this lady ask thy advice as to the wisdom of the loan?"

"Quite otherwise. She had pictured to herself this son of hers as a wealthy and powerful man of Babylon. To suggest the contrary was to infuriate her. A fair rebuke I had. I knew the risk for this inexperienced boy, but as she offered security I could not refuse her.

"This," continued Mathon, waving a bit of pack rope tied into a knot, "belongs to Nebatur, the camel trader. When he would buy a herd larger than his funds, he brings to me this knot, and I lend to him according to his needs. He is a wise trader. I have confidence in his good judgment and can lend him freely. Many other merchants of Babylon have my confidence because of their honorable behavior. Their tokens come and go frequently in my token box. Good merchants are an asset to our city, and it profits me to aid them to keep trade moving, that Babylon be prosperous."

Mathon picked out a beetle carved in turquoise and tossed it contemptuously on the floor. "A bug from Egypt. The lad who owns this does not care whether I ever receive back my gold. When I reproach him he replies, 'How can

I repay when ill fate pursues me? You have plenty more.' What can I do? The token is his father's, a worthy man of small means who did pledge his land and herd to back his son's enterprises.

"The youth found success at first and then was overzealous to gain great wealth. His knowledge was immature. His enterprises collapsed. Youth is ambitious. Youth would take short cuts to wealth and the desirable things for which it stands. To secure wealth quickly youth often borrows unwisely.

"Youth, never having had experience, cannot realize that hopeless debt is like a deep pit into which one may descend quickly and where one may struggle vainly for many days. It is a pit of sorrow and regrets, where the brightness of the sun is overcast and night is made unhappy by restless sleeping.

"Yet I do not discourage borrowing gold. I encourage it. I recommend it if it be for a wise purpose. I myself made my first real success as a merchant with borrowed gold.

"Yet what should the lender do in such a case? The youth is in despair and accomplishes nothing. He is discouraged. He makes no effort to repay. My heart turns against depriving the father of his land and cattle."

"You tell me much that I am interested to hear," ventured Rodan, "but I hear no answer to my question. Should I lend my fifty pieces of gold to my sister's husband? They mean much to me."

"Thy sister is a sterling woman whom I do much esteem. Should her husband come to me and ask to borrow fifty pieces of gold, I should ask him for what purpose he would use it. If he answered that he desired to become a merchant like myself and deal in jewels and rich furnishings, I would say, 'What knowledge have you of the ways of trade? Do you know where you can buy at lowest cost? Do you know where you can sell at a fair price?' Could he say yes to these questions?"

"No, he could not," Rodan admitted. "He has helped me much in making spears, and he has helped some in the shops."

"Then would I say to him that his purpose was not wise. Merchants must learn their trade. His ambition, though worthy, is not practical, and I would not lend him any gold. But, supposing he could say, 'Yes, I have helped merchants much. I know how to travel to Smyrna and to buy at low cost the rugs the housewives weave. I also know many of the rich people of Babylon to whom I can sell these at a large profit.'

"Then I would say, 'Your purpose is wise and your ambition honorable. I shall be glad to lend you the fifty pieces of gold if you can give me security that they will be returned.' But would he say, 'I have no security other than that I am an honored man and will pay you well for the loan,' then would I reply, 'I treasure much each piece of gold. Were the robbers to take it from you as you journeyed to Smyrna or take the rugs from you as you returned, then you would have no means of repaying me, and my gold would be gone.'

"Gold, you see, Rodan, is the merchandise of the lender of money. It is easy to lend. If it is lent unwisely, then it is difficult to get back. The wise lender wishes not the risk of the undertaking but the guarantee of safe repayment.

"'Tis well," he continued, "to assist those that are in trouble. 'Tis well to help those upon whom fate has laid a heavy hand, 'tis well to help those who are starting, that they may progress and become valuable citizens. But help must be given wisely, lest, like the farmer's ass, in our desire to help we but take upon ourselves the burden that belongs to another.

"Again I wandered from thy question, Rodan, but hear my answer. Keep thy fifty pieces of gold. What thy labor earns for thee and what is given thee for reward is thine own, and no man can put an obligation upon thee to part with it unless it do be thy wish. If thee wouldst lend it so that it may earn thee more gold, then lend with caution and in many places. I like not idle gold; even less I like too much of risk. How many years hast thou labored as a spearmaker?"

"Fully three."

"How much besides the king's gift hast saved?"

"Three gold pieces."

"Each year that thou hast labored, thou has denied thyself good things to save from thine earnings one piece of gold?"

"'Tis as you say."

"Then mightest save in fifty years of labor fifty pieces of gold by thy self-denial?"

"A lifetime of labor it would be."

"Thinkest thou thy sister would wish to jeopardize the savings of fifty years of labor over the bronze melting pot that her husband might experiment on being a merchant?"

"Not if I spoke in your words."

"Then go to her and say, 'Three years I have labored each day except fast days, from morning until night, and I have denied myself many things that my heart craved. For each year of labor and self-denial, I have to show one piece of gold. Thou art my favored sister, and I wish that thy husband may engage in business in which he will prosper greatly. If he will submit to me a plan that seems wise and possible to my friend Mathon, then will I gladly lend to him my savings of an entire year, that he may have an opportunity to prove that he can succeed.'

"Do that, I say, and if he has within him the soul to succeed, he can prove it. If he fails, he will not owe thee more than he can hope someday to repay. I am a gold lender because I own more gold than I can use in my own trade. I desire my surplus gold to labor for others and thereby earn more gold. I do not wish to take the risk of losing my gold, for I have labored much and denied myself much to secure it. Therefore I will no longer lend any of it where I am not confident that it is safe and will be returned to me. Neither will I lend it where I am not convinced that its earnings will be promptly paid to me.

"I have told to thee, Rodan, a few of the secrets of my token chest. From them you may understand the weakness of men and their eagerness to borrow that which they have no certain means to repay. From this you can see how often their high hopes of the great earnings they could make, if they but had gold, are but false hopes they have not the ability or training to fulfill.

"Thou, Rodan, now have gold, which thou shouldst put to earning more gold for thee. Thou art about to become even as I, a gold lender. If thou dost safely preserve thy treasure, it will produce liberal earnings for thee and be a rich source of pleasure and profit during all thy days, but if thou dost let it escape from thee, it will be a source of constant sorrow and regret as long as thy memory doth last. What desirest thou most of this gold in thy wallet?"

"To keep it safe."

"Wisely spoken," replied Mathon approvingly. "Thy first desire is for safety. Thinkest thou that in the custody of thy sister's husband it would be truly safe from possible loss?"

"I fear not, for he is not wise in guarding gold."

"Then be not swayed by foolish sentiments of obligation to trust thy treasure to any person. If thou wouldst help thy family or thy friends, find other ways than risking the loss of thy treasure. Forget not that gold slippeth away in unexpected ways from those unskilled in guarding it. As well waste thy treasure in extravagance as let others lose it for thee. What next after safety dost desire of this treasure of thine?"

"That it earn more gold."

"Again thou speakest with wisdom. It should be made to earn and grow larger. Gold wisely lent may even double itself with its earnings before a man like you groweth old. If you risk losing it, you risk losing all that it would earn as well.

"Therefore be not swayed by the fantastic plans of impractical men who think they see ways to force thy gold to make earnings unusually large. Such plans are the creations of dreamers unskilled in the safe and dependable laws of trade. Be conservative in what thou expect it to earn, that thou mayest keep and enjoy thy treasure. To hire it out with a promise of usurious returns is to invite loss.

"Seek to associate thyself with men and enterprises whose success is established, that thy treasure may earn liberally under their skillful use and be guarded safely by their wisdom and experience. Thus mayest thou avoid the misfortunes that follow most of the sons of men to whom the gods see fit to entrust gold."

When Rodan would thank him for his wise advice, he would not listen, saying, "The king's gift shall teach thee much wisdom. If wouldst keep thy fifty pieces of gold, thou must be discreet indeed. Many uses will tempt thee. Much advice will be spoken to thee. Numerous opportunities to make large profits will be offered thee. The stories from my token box should warn thee before thou lettest any piece of gold, leave thy pouch to be sure that thou hast a safe way to pull it back again. Should my further advice appeal to thee, return again. It is gladly given. Ere thou goest, read this which I have carved beneath the lid of my token box. It applies equally to the borrower and the lender:

*"Better a little caution than a great regret."*

# ◆ Dan ◆

In this part of the story, Rodan the spearmaker came into fifty pieces of gold. He was asked to lend it to his sister's husband, but he was not sure. So he went to visit Mathon, who was a gold lender. This is a great example of getting advice from an expert.

Mathon said, "Gold bringeth unto its possessor responsibility and a changed position in regard to his fellow men. It bringeth the fear lest he lose it or it be tricked away from him. It bringeth a feeling of power and ability to do good. Likewise, it bringeth opportunities whereby his very good intentions may bring him into difficulties."

If you've ever received a substantial amount of money, an inheritance, a settlement, or the sale of something large, you can relate. Money changes your position with your family and friends. On the one hand, you get scared you're going to lose it, or someone will trick you into giving it away, but on the other hand, you feel powerful. It's quite a feeling to walk into a store that you frequent and know that you could afford anything in the place.

As Mathon said, sometimes your good intentions are the very things that can cause you problems with money. The truth is, when you achieve your goal of becoming wealthy, your relationships are going to change.

Anthony Robbins shares a story about when he was first starting out. He wanted to buy a castle, but all of his family and friends were telling him not to do it. He had been holding himself back financially and from becoming all that he wanted to become, because he was afraid of what other people would think.

Finally one day he decided to stop worrying so much about what others thought. He knew that his real friends would support him no matter what. Author Wayne Dyer calls this becoming independent of the good opinion of other people, and you know what? Once Tony stopped holding himself back, he became the Tony Robbins success story that we all know today.

Here's another story that's not as well known. It's about author Marshall Goldsmith, author of *Take It to the Next Level*, and a friend of mine. My friend was at Marshall's house several years ago, when he was on the cusp of the huge success that he's since experienced.

Marshall was already successful and was one of the top ten management consultants in the world. He had a big beautiful home in Rancho Santa Fe, California, and owned several classic cars and a thriving business. But Marshall was concerned about the impact of his wealth and his success on his kids. He said to my friend, "Do you think there's a way to raise kids in the midst of all this wealth and still have my kids turn out as good, honest, decent, people?"

My friend and Marshall spent quite a bit of time discussing it that day. Now Brian and Kelly, Marshall's children, did grow up to be well-balanced, grounded people, so it's definitely possible, but the story just goes to prove that even supersuccessful people still worry about how wealth will change them.

So your first exercise for this chapter is to write down some of the fears you've had about how being wealthy will change your relationships. Will your spouse become threatened? Are you worried your kids will get spoiled? Maybe your poor friends will start to try and mooch off you. Write your thoughts in your journal.

Now take a look at what you've just written. It's a lot easier to deal with our fears when we can see them in black-and-white. We'll get to some techniques for eliminating these fears in a later chapter.

In our story, Rodan wanted to know if people really did pay back loans. Mathon showed him the chest of tokens that he collected from people who borrowed gold from him. In modern terms, we call it *collateral*. It's something that you put down to show that you'll pay back the loan. Otherwise the lender can keep the valuable item instead.

Mathon said, "The safest loans are those whose possessions are of more value than the one they desire. They own lands or jewels or camels or other things that could be sold to repay the loan." Safe loans are those of the one who had the capacity to learn. They labor or serve, and repay. They have income, and if they are honest and suffer no misfortune, they also repay. These loans are based on human efforts.

He's saying it's safest to lend money to people who have other assets that could be sold to repay the loan. In the last chapter, we went over what a real asset is, so if you're going to lend some money to people, you need to make sure that they are putting up a real asset that they actually own and that is worth more than what you are lending them.

Alternatively, you can lend money to people who have the capacity to earn it, who have a steady job and an honest character. Your gullible brother who wants to borrow some money to invest in the latest scheme is probably not the best person to lend money to.

Mathon said it this way: "Be not swayed by foolish sentiments of obligation to trust thy treasure to any person. If thou wouldst help thy family or thy friends, find other ways than risking the loss of thy treasure. Forget not that gold slippeth away in unexpected ways from those unskilled in guarding it. As well waste thy treasure in extravagance as let others lose it for thee."

He's saying that no matter how cute your teenage daughter is, it's probably not a good idea to lend her the money for a car, because you're probably not going to see that money again. You can find other ways to help her get a car, but giving her a loan is not a good plan.

Mathon said you might as well go out and blow the money on something extravagant rather than let someone else lose your money for you. Yes, it's tough to tell family members that you won't lend to them, but you have to be willing to do the tough things to protect your money. Remember, money is counting on you to protect it, so use it wisely. As has been said, better a little caution than a great regret.

Now for your exercise. You're going to do a little imaginary role playing. As we said, it can be hard to tell someone no when it comes to lending him or her money, so it's a good idea to practice it so that the words don't sound like a foreign language when they come out of your mouth.

Actually say out loud what you'd say if your favorite relative asked to borrow money but you needed to say no. It might sound like this: "Peter, I've considered what you've said, but I really don't think it's a good idea at this time. Is there another way I can help you out that doesn't involve a loan?"

Be sure to put it in the name of one of your favorite relatives instead of *Peter* (unless your favorite relative is named Peter, of course).

There's one other consideration. The person you've just said no to is probably going to be mad. That's to be expected. Some people use anger to try to get what they want. You have to be prepared for that and disengage from their anger. It's better to have people mad at you than to make them a loan that they won't pay back so that the relationship gets ruined. It's better to say no when you need to, no matter how hard it is.

Now let's talk a little bit about if you're the borrower. What are some things that you can do to be a good candidate for a loan? First of all, you need to make sure that you're borrowing money for the right reasons. Make sure that you need the money for something essential, not just for something you want. It's better to save the money for things that are optional and pay cash for them.

Second, you need to have good credit. We'll talk more about debt and credit in a later chapter, but for now, let's just say that if you have an established credit history with a track record of paying your loans off in a timely manner, a lender is far more likely to want to lend to you again.

It's a good idea to have some kind of asset that you can use as collateral. Again, you don't want to try to leverage something you don't own to get a loan. Your whole house of cards may come crashing down around you.

Just stick to the simple principles you're learning here. If you don't have any assets yet, you can still get a loan if you have a good job and a steady income, but if you have a lot of other debt, it won't work.

Most importantly, you have to have integrity. Don't go running up credit cards and then declaring bankruptcy. Take your obligations seriously. Remember, money is watching you, and if you respect it, money will come to you. If you abuse it, it's going to leave.

## Babylon Builder

In this chapter, we talked about what happens when you become wealthy. It changes your relationships, but even the most successful people have had the same fears as you do. Once they decided to stop holding themselves back, their success skyrocketed. We also learned about loaning money, how to loan it to, and whom *not* to loan money to.

Finally, we talked about how to be a good borrower if you're the one who has to borrow some money. For action steps, you wrote down some of your fears about what being wealthy will do to your relationships, and you practiced the difficult conversation of saying no to lending money to someone you love.

# EIGHT
# The Walls
# of Babylon

Old Banzar, grim warrior of another day, stood guard at the passageway leading to the top of the ancient walls of Babylon. Up above, valiant defenders were battling to hold the walls. Upon them depended the future existence of this great city with its hundreds of thousands of citizens. Over the walls came the roar of the attacking armies, the yelling of many men, the trampling of thousands of horses, the deafening boom of the battering rams pounding the bronze gates.

In the street behind the gate lounged the spearmen, waiting to defend the entrance should the gates give way. They were but few for the task. The main armies of Babylon were with their king, far away in the east on the great expedition against the Elamites. No attack upon the city having been anticipated during their absence, the defending forces were small. Unexpectedly, from the north, bore down the mighty armies of the Assyrians, and now the walls must hold or Babylon was doomed.

About Banzar were great crowds of citizens, white-faced and terrified, eagerly seeking news of the battle. With hushed awe, they viewed the stream of wounded and dead being carried or led out of the passageway. Here was the crucial point of attack. After three days of circling about the city, the enemy had suddenly thrown his great strength against this section and this gate.

The defenders from the top of the wall fought off the climbing platforms and the scaling ladders of the attackers with arrows, burning oil, and if any reached the top, spears. Against the defenders, thousands of the enemy's archers poured a deadly barrage of arrows.

Old Banzar had the vantage point for news. He was closest to the conflict and first to hear of each fresh repulse of the frenzied attackers. An elderly merchant crowded close to him, his palsied hands quivering. "Tell me, tell me," he pleaded. "They cannot get in. My sons are with the good king. There is no one to protect my old wife. My goods, they will steal all. My food, they will leave nothing. We are old, too old to defend ourselves, too old for slaves. We shall starve. We shall die. Tell me they cannot get in."

"Calm thyself, good merchant," the guard responded. "The walls of Babylon are strong. Go back to the bazaar and tell your wife that the walls will protect you and all of your possessions as safely as they protect the rich treasures of the king. Keep close to the walls, lest the arrows flying over strike you."

A woman with a babe in arms took the old man's place as he withdrew. "Sergeant, what news from the top? Tell

me truly, that I may reassure my poor husband. He lies
with fever from his terrible wounds, yet insists upon his
armor and his spear to protect me, who am with child.
Terrible he says will be the vengeful lust of our enemies
should they break in."

"Be thou of good heart, thou mother that is and is
again to be. The walls of Babylon will protect you and your
babes. They are high and strong. Hear ye not the yells
of our valiant defenders as they empty the cauldrons of
burning oil upon the ladder scalers?"

"Yes, that do I hear, and also the roar of the battering
rams that do hammer at our gates."

"Back to thy husband. Tell him the gates are strong
and withstand the rams. Also that the scalers climb the
walls but to receive the waiting spear thrust. Watch thy
way and hasten behind yon buildings."

Banzar stepped aside to clear the passage for heavily
armed reinforcements. As with clanking bronze shields
and heavy tread they tramped by, a small girl plucked at
his girdle. "Tell me please, soldier, are we safe? I hear the
awful noises. I see the men all bleeding. I am so frightened. What will become of our family, of my mother, little
brother, and the baby?"

The grim old campaigner blinked his eyes and thrust
forward his chin as he beheld the child. "Be not afraid,
little one," he reassured her. "The walls of Babylon will
protect you and mother and little brother and the baby.
It was for the safety of such as you that the good Queen
Semiramis built them over a hundred years ago. Never
have they been broken through. Go back and tell your

mother and little brother and the baby that the walls of Babylon will protect them and they need have no fear."

Day after day, old Banzar stood at his post and watched the reinforcements file up the passageway, there to stay and fight until wounded or dead they came down once more. Around him, unceasingly crowded the throngs of frightened citizens eagerly seeking to learn if the walls would hold. To all he gave his answer with the fine dignity of an old soldier, "The walls of Babylon will protect you."

For three weeks and five days the attack waged with scarcely ceasing violence. Harder and grimmer set the jaw of Banzar as the passage behind, wet with the blood of the many wounded, was churned into mud by the never ceasing streams of men passing up and staggering down. Each day the slaughtered attackers piled up in heaps before the wall. Each night they were carried back and buried by their comrades.

Upon the fifth night of the fourth week, the clamor without diminished. The first streaks of daylight, illuminating the plains, disclosed great clouds of dust raised by the retreating armies.

A mighty shout went up from the defenders. There was no mistaking its meaning. It was repeated by the waiting troops behind the walls. It was echoed by the citizens upon the streets. It swept over the city with the violence of a storm.

People rushed from the houses. The streets were jammed with a throbbing mob. The pent-up fear of weeks found an outlet in the wild chorus of joy. From the top of the high tower of the Temple of Bel burst forth the flames of victory. Skyward floated the column of blue smoke to carry the message far and wide.

The walls of Babylon had once again repulsed a mighty and vicious foe determined to loot her rich treasures and to ravish and enslave her citizens. Babylon endured century after century because it was fully protected. It could not afford to be otherwise. The walls of Babylon were an outstanding example of man's need and desire for protection.

This desire is inherent in the human race. It is just as strong today as it ever was, but we have developed broader and better plans to accomplish the same purpose.

In this day, behind the impregnable walls of insurance, savings accounts, and dependable investments, we can guard ourselves against the unexpected tragedies that may enter any door and seat themselves before any fireside. We cannot afford to be without adequate protection.

---

## ❧ Dan ❧

This chapter is a story of an epic battle. In this story, the king of Babylon had taken his army to fight with the neighboring country. The pain, fear, and disappointment of war are described in detail. The war lasted almost a month, and then on the fifth night of the fourth week, the war ended.

In this story, the walls of Babylon are compared to man's desire for protection. This desire is inherent in the human race. Behind our savings accounts and dependable walls of insurance, we can guard ourselves against the unexpected tragedies that can happen to us. At the last part of the story, the lesson is we cannot afford to be without adequate protection.

Let's talk about protection a bit, specifically insurance. While it's good to have insurance, you certainly don't want to have too much insurance or the wrong kinds.

In "Transforming Debt into Wealth," John Cummuta talks about insurance. He says

> Insurance companies don't lose money on their insurance business. Sure, a small number of insurance companies go out of business because they make bad outside investments, but they do not lose money on their insurance programs. When they sell you an insurance policy, they're gambling with the odds in their favor that bad things will not happen to you, and you—silly, if you think about it—are gambling that bad things will happen to you.
>
> Insurance companies never lose at this game. Sure, there are a small number of people who file big claims after paying only a few premiums, but while it may appear that the insurance company loses money in these situations, the fact is that they have thousands of other people paying premiums to whom nothing bad is happening, so they simply take the profit they're making on most people and easily cover the benefits they have to pay out to the few unfortunate ones. Insurers know that you are thousands of times more likely to be

one of the fortunate ones who cost them nothing and make them tons of profit.

How does all of this apply to your insurance? Let's start with life insurance. The purpose of life insurance is not to make your survivors rich should you die. It is to assure them of the continuation of your income stream should you stop producing it yourself. For most people, the most cost-efficient way to accomplish this is to buy term life insurance with a sufficient death benefit amount that the total return would equal your present monthly income times however many years the term is for.

Frankly, once your gold starts multiplying on its own, you probably won't need life insurance anymore. You'll have enough assets that your income can be replaced without having to pay insurance premiums. Until then—term life insurance. After your passive income stream is sufficient to go on after you aren't around, you can cancel it.

How do you find a good life-insurance company? If you're happy with the company that provides your other insurance, get a quote from them. In addition, contact your state's insurance department for a list of companies licensed in your state. Then here are the steps.

Number one, ask friends and relatives for recommendations based on their own experiences. Two, talk to an insurance agent or broker. Three, conduct an Internet search, and four, research companies at the public library.

The most important thing to take away about life insurance is that it shouldn't be considered a form of investment to make your heirs rich. It's to cover the income you'd have

earned had you lived, should you pass away while you depen-
dents still need it.

What about auto insurance? If you passively accept all the
coverages and deductible levels your insurance agent offers
in their "standard package," you could end up paying hundreds of dollars a year more than you need to. For example,
the medical coverage on your car insurance policy is probably redundant with portions of your health insurance. You
likely already have a medical health insurance policy that
covers you and your family both in and out of the car twenty-
four hours a day. Nondependents who might be hurt in your
vehicle would likely be taken care of by the liability portion of
your policy, so if you have a solid health-insurance package,
the medical coverages on your car insurance may well be
unnecessary. Of course, before taking any action, be sure to
review your policy with your agent.

Your agent may also recommend road service and rental
car coverages, but you'll probably never even remember you
have them should you ever get into the highly unlikely situations in which these coverages actually apply. Most people
have an outside auto service like AAA. Why pay twice?

Your action step for auto insurance is to shop around. Car
insurance is a very competitive business, and you can easily
get quotes from different companies that might end up saving you hundreds of dollars a year in premiums. One place
where you can do this is through www.insweb.com.

The last type of insurance we'll look at here is medical
insurance. This is a very hot topic in the news at present.
It's a political issue that has people from both sides arguing
passionately. Regardless of how the health-care system is set

up, or how the medical-insurance programs are managed, or of any of the issues up for debate right now, there are some things you can do to make sure that you're not overpaying for medical insurance.

If you paid for all or part of your medical or health insurance coverage yourself, take the highest possible deductible you can stand. Unless you or a family member is particularly prone to illness, all you really need medical insurance for is to protect you from the huge bills that can come from a major illness or injury. These are the huge bills that could drain your savings and investments.

If you insist on having a coverage level that will pay for every sniffle, you will likely pay through the nose in the form of higher monthly premiums. In most cases, the increased premiums you'll pay over a year for a lower deductible will cost you more than carrying a higher deductible and covering your incidental medical expenses yourself.

Another core element is to stay as healthy as possible. If you don't smoke, don't abuse alcohol or drugs, maintain a healthy weight, and don't eat a lot of junk, you're less likely to come down with some kind of preventable illness. What's the old adage? An ounce of prevention is worth a pound of cure. That's never been more true than today.

The bottom line is to look at insurance the same way you do any other investment of your gold. Take the advice of experts, but use your own mind too. Insurance laws vary from state to state, so be sure and discuss any changes with your insurance advisor.

In fact, that's your first exercise of this chapter. Make an appointment with your insurance advisors, or advisors if you have different companies for different insurances, to have a look at your insurance premiums.

Go over your life insurance, auto insurance, and health insurance. Make sure you're adequately covered but not overcovered either.

Now let's take a different look at the metaphor of the walls of Babylon. If we look at it another way, the walls of Babylon can be compared to our minds. It's not easy to change our thinking to that of a wealthy mind-set. It's no coincidence that the war in our story lasted about a month. Why a month?

George Clason could have written of a war that lasted several months or even several years. Why did he pick that length of time? Because that's about how long it takes to change your thought patterns. When you first start implementing the ideas in this program, your old patterns are going to fight hard for their existence.

Remember the exercise in which you listed your fears about how money will change your relationships? When you start to become wealthy, there's likely to be a war inside your mind. You're probably used to worrying about money, panicking about money, stressing out about money. When you finally have a lot of money, is that going to change, or will you start worrying about how not to lose it?

Money and money worries are part of our modern culture. It's more acceptable to say, "I'm stressed out about money," than it is to say, "I don't have a care in the world financially."

There is a big difference between worrying about money and having money problems, but most of us fall into the category of worrying about money. Regardless of income, most people just don't feel particularly good about their financial status, but worrying about money is never a solution to a money problem.

Today, in addition to worrying about their personal financial situations, many people are worried about how their finances could be devastated by a natural disaster, a terrorist attack, a new national economic policy, a major corporate decision, or a major correction in our ever-changing financial markets. These are the modern wars we face, not only within the walls of Babylon.

So let's do an exercise. Get your journal and answer these questions. How often do you worry about money? Nonstop? Once a day? Once a week? What impact is this worrying is having on your life? Write your answers now.

In reality, these worries are only thoughts. This war is being fought in between the walls of your skull. If you're going to change your financial picture to being one of a wealthy person, you're going to need to stop worrying about money.

How can you do this? Whenever you start to feel fear or be afraid of something to do with money, remind yourself that it's only a thought, and then change your thought to something more empowering.

Reassure yourself that you're following the Laws of Gold and are implementing the Seven Cures for a Lean Purse. Everything is going to be OK.

This is your last exercise for this chapter. Write down in your journal several positive statements and thoughts you can use when you need to change a negative money thought to a positive one.

For example, when you think, "I'm not going to have enough money to pay my bills this month," change that to, "Eventually they'll get paid. Let's look at which ones I can pay now." Or, "My stock portfolio is going down. I'm going to lose all my money." Change that thought to, "I've lost the money only if I sell the stock. I need to talk to investment advisor about whether or not I should sell it or hang on to it."

See, you're transforming your money worries into positive thoughts and actions. You're not denying reality; you're just changing it into something productive.

### Babylon Builder

In this chapter, we learned all about protection. We learned about having financial protection with things like insurance and savings. We learned about how to make wise investments in life, auto, and health insurance. We also talked more about money worries and how to change your thinking from negative worrying to productive action. You took several actions in this chapter. You made appointments to review your insurance coverage, and you made a list of your financial worries and came up with empowering thoughts you can think instead. You are now prepared to win the battle going on inside your head.

# NINE
# The Camel Trader
# of Babylon

The hungrier one becomes, the clearer one's mind works—also the more sensitive one becomes to the odors of food.

Tarkad, the son of Azure, certainly thought so. For two whole days he had tasted no food except two small figs purloined from over the wall of a garden. Not another could he grab before the angry woman rushed forth and chased him down the street. Her shrill cries were still ringing in his ears as he walked through the marketplace. They helped him to restrain his restless fingers from snatching the tempting fruits from the baskets of the market women. Never before had he realized how much food was brought to the markets of Babylon and how good it smelled.

Leaving the market, he walked across to the inn and paced back and forth in front of the eating house. Perhaps here he might meet someone he knew, someone from whom he could borrow a copper that would gain him a smile from the unfriendly keeper of the inn and with it a liberal helping. Without the copper he knew all too well how unwelcome he would be.

In his abstraction, he unexpectedly found himself face to face with the one man he wished most to avoid, the tall, bony figure of Dabasir, the camel trader. Of all the friends and others from whom he had borrowed small sums, Dabasir made him feel the most uncomfortable because of his failure to keep his promises to repay promptly.

Dabasir's face lighted up at the sight of him. "Ha. 'Tis Tarkad, just the one I have been seeking, that he might repay the two pieces of copper which I lent him a moon ago; also the piece of silver which I lent to him before that. We are well met. I can make good use of the coins this very day. What say, boy? What say?"

Tarkad stuttered, and his face flushed. He had naught in his empty stomach to nerve him to argue with the out-spoken Dabasir. "I am sorry, very sorry," he mumbled weakly, "but this day I have neither the copper nor the silver with which I could repay."

"Then get it," Dabasir insisted. "Surely thou canst get hold of a few coppers and a piece of silver to repay the generosity of an old friend of thy father who aided thee when thou wast in need?"

"'Tis because ill fortune does pursue me that I cannot pay."

"Ill fortune! Wouldst blame the gods for thine own weakness? Ill fortune pursues every man who thinks more of borrowing than of repaying. Come with me, boy, while I eat. I am hungry, and I would tell thee a tale."

Tarkad flinched from the brutal frankness of Dabasir, but here at least was an invitation to enter the coveted doorway of the eating house. Dabasir pushed him to a far corner of the room, where they seated themselves upon small rugs.

When Kauskor, the proprietor, appeared smiling, Dabasir addressed him with his usual freedom. "Fat lizard of the desert, bring to me a leg of the goat, very brown, with much juice, and bread and all of the vegetables, for I am hungry and want much food. Do not forget my friend here. Bring to him a jug of water. Have it cooled, for the day is hot."

Tarkad's heart sank. Must he sit here and drink water while he watched this man devour an entire goat leg? He said nothing. He thought of nothing he could say.

Dabasir, however, knew no such thing as silence. Smiling and waving his hand good-naturedly to the other customers, all of whom knew him, he continued. "I did hear from a traveler just returned from Urfa of a certain rich man who has a piece of stone cut so thin that one can look through it. He put it in the window of his house to keep out the rains. It is yellow, so this traveler does relate, and he was permitted to look through it, and all the outside world looked strange and not like it really is. What say you to that, Tarkad? Thinkest all the world could look to a man a different color from what it is?"

"I dare say," responded the youth, much more interested in the fat leg of goat placed before Dabasir.

"Well, I know it to be true, for I myself have seen the world all of a different color from what it really is, and the tale I am about to tell relates how I came to see it in its right color once more."

"Dabasir will tell a tale," whispered a neighboring diner to his neighbor, and dragged his rug close. Other diners brought their food and crowded in a semicircle. They crunched noisily in the ears of Tarkad and brushed him with their meaty bones. He alone was without food. Dabasir did not offer to share with him nor even motion him to a small corner of the hard bread that was broken off and had fallen from the platter to the floor.

"The tale that I am about to tell," began Dabasir, pausing to bite a goodly chunk from the goat leg, "relates to my early life and how I came to be a camel trader. Did anyone know that I once was a slave in Syria?"

A murmur of surprise ran through the audience, to which Dabasir listened with satisfaction. "When I was a young man," continued Dabasir after another vicious onslaught on the goat leg, "I learned the trade of my father, the making of saddles. I worked with him in his shop and took to myself a wife. Being young and not greatly skilled, I could earn but little, just enough to support my excellent wife in a modest way.

"I craved good things, which I could not afford. Soon I found that the shopkeepers would trust me to pay later even though I could not pay at the time. Being young and without experience, I did not know that he who spends more than he earns is sowing the winds of needless self-indulgence, from which he is sure to reap the whirlwinds of trouble and humiliation.

"So I indulged my whims for fine raiment and bought luxuries for my good wife and our home beyond our means. I paid as I could, and for a while all went well, but in time I discovered I could not use my earnings both to live upon and to pay my debts. Creditors began to pursue me to pay for my extravagant purchases, and my life became miserable. I borrowed from my friends but could not repay them either. Things went from bad to worse. My wife returned to her father, and I decided to leave Babylon and seek another city, where a young man might have better chances.

"For two years I had a restless and unsuccessful life working for caravan traders. From this I fell in with a set of likable robbers who scoured the desert for unarmed caravans. Such deeds were unworthy of the son of my father, but I was seeing the world through a colored stone and did not realize to what degradation I had fallen.

"We met with success on our first trip, capturing a rich haul of gold and silks and valuable merchandise. This loot we took to Ginir and squandered.

"The second time we were not so fortunate. Just after we had made our capture, we were attacked by the spearsmen of a native chief whom the caravans paid for protection. Our two leaders were killed, and the rest of us were taken to Damascus, where we were stripped of our clothing and sold as slaves.

"I was purchased for two pieces of silver by a Syrian desert chief. With my hair shorn and but a loincloth to wear, I was not so different from the other slaves. Being a reckless youth, I thought it merely an adventure until my master took me before his four wives and told them they could have me for a eunuch.

"Then indeed did I realize the hopelessness of my situation. These men of the desert were fierce and warlike. I was subject to their will without weapons or means of escape.

"Fearful I stood, as those four women looked me over. I wondered if I could expect pity from them. Sira, the first wife, was older than the others. Her face was impassive as she looked upon me. I turned from her with little consolation. The next was a contemptuous beauty who gazed at me as indifferently, as if I had been a worm of the earth. The two younger ones tittered as though it were all an exciting joke.

"It seemed an age that I stood waiting sentence. Each woman appeared willing for the others to decide. Finally Sira spoke up in a cold voice. 'Of eunuchs we have plenty, but of camel tenders we have few, and they are a worthless lot. Even this day I would visit my mother, who is sick with the fever, and there is no slave I would trust to lead my camel. Ask this slave if he can lead a camel.'

"My master thereupon questioned me, 'What know you of camels?' Striving to conceal my eagerness, I replied, 'I can make them kneel, I can load them, I can lead them on long trips without tiring. If need be, I can repair their trappings.'

"'The slave speaks forward enough,' observed my master. 'If thou so desire, Sira, take this man for thy camel tender.'

"So I was turned over to Sira, and that day I led her camel upon a long journey to her sick mother. I took the occasion to thank her for her intercession and also to tell her that I was not a slave by birth, but the son of a free man, an honorable saddlemaker of Babylon. I also told her much of my story. Her comments were disconcerting to me, and I pondered much afterwards on what she said.

"'How can you call yourself a free man when your weakness has brought you to this? If a man has in himself the soul of a slave, will he not become one no matter what his birth, even as water seeks its level? If a man has within him the soul of a free man, will he not become respected and honored in his own city in spite of his misfortune?'

"For over a year I was a slave and lived with the slaves, but I could not become as one of them. One day Sira asked me, 'In the eventime, when the other slaves can mingle and enjoy the society of each other, why dost thou sit in thy tent alone?'

"To which I responded, 'I am pondering what you have said to me. I wonder if I have the soul of a slave. I cannot join them, so I must sit apart.'

"'I too must sit apart. My dowry was large, and my lord married me because of it. Yet he does not desire me. What every woman longs for is to be desired. Because of this, and because I am barren and have neither son nor daughter, must I sit apart. Were I a man I would rather die than be such a slave, but the conventions of our tribe make slaves of women.'

"'What think thou of me by this time?' I asked her suddenly. 'Have I the soul of a man, or have I the soul of a slave?'

"'Have you a desire to repay the just debts you owe in Babylon?'

"'Yes, I have the desire, but I see no way.'

"'If thou contentedly let the years slip by and made no effort to repay, then thou hast but the contemptible soul of a slave. No man is otherwise who cannot respect himself, and no man can respect himself who does not repay honest debts.'

"'But what can I do who am a slave in Syria?'

"'Stay a slave in Syria, thou weakling.'

"'I am not a weakling,' I denied hotly.

"'Then prove it.'

"'How?'

"'Does not thy great king fight his enemies in every way he can and with every force he has? Thy debts are thine enemies. They ran thee out of Babylon. You left them alone, and they grew too strong for thee. Hadst fought them as a man, thou couldst have conquered them and been one honored among the townspeople, but thou had not the soul to fight them, and behold, thy pride hast gone down until thou art a slave in Syria.'

"Much I thought over her unkind accusations and many defensive phrases I worded to prove myself not a slave at heart, but I was not to have the chance to use them. Three days later the maid of Sira took me to her mistress.

"'My mother is again very sick. Saddle the two best camels in my husband's herd. Tie on water skins and saddlebags for a long journey. The maid will give thee food at the kitchen tent.'

"I packed the camels, wondering much at the quantity of provisions the maid provided, for the mother dwelt less than a day's journey away. The maid rode the rear camel, which followed, and I led the camel of my mistress. When we reached her mother's house, it was just dark. Sira dismissed the maid and said to me, 'Dabasir, hast thou the soul of a free man or the soul of a slave?'

"'The soul of a free man,' I insisted.

"'Now is thy chance to prove it. Thy master hath imbibed deeply, and his chiefs are in a stupor. Take then these camels and make thy escape. Here in this bag is raiment of thy master's to disguise thee. I will say thou stoledst the camels and ran away while I visited my sick mother.'

"'Thou hast the soul of a queen,' I told her. 'Much do I wish that I might lead thee to happiness.'

"'Happiness awaits not the runaway wife who seeks it in far lands among strange people. Go thine own way, and may the gods of the desert protect thee, for the way is far and barren of food or water.'

"I needed no further urging, but thanked her warmly and was away into the night. I knew not this strange country and had only a dim idea of the direction in which lay Babylon, but struck out bravely across the desert toward the hills. One camel I rode, and the other I led. All that night I traveled and all the next day, urged on by the knowledge of the terrible fate that was meted out to slaves who stole their master's property and tried to escape.

"Late that afternoon, I reached a rough country as uninhabitable as the desert. The sharp rocks bruised the feet of my faithful camels, and soon they were picking their way slowly and painfully along. I met neither man nor beast and could well understand why they shunned this inhospitable land.

"It was such a journey from then on as few men live to tell of. Day after day we plodded along. Food and water gave out. The heat of the sun was merciless. At the end of the ninth day, I slid from the back of my mount with the feeling that I was too weak to ever remount and I would surely die, lost in this abandoned country.

"I stretched out upon the ground and slept, not waking until the first gleam of daylight. I sat up and looked about me. There was a coolness in the morning air. My camels lay dejected not far away. About me was a vast waste of broken country covered with rock and sand and thorny things, no sign of water, naught to eat for man or camel.

"Could it be that in this peaceful quiet I faced my end? My mind was clearer than it had ever been before. My body now seemed of little importance. My parched and bleeding lips, my dry and swollen tongue, my empty stomach all had lost their supreme agonies of the day before.

"I looked across into the uninviting distance, and once again came to me the question, 'Have I the soul of a slave or the soul of a free man?' Then with clearness I realized that if I had the soul of a slave, I should give up, lie down in the desert, and die—a fitting end for a runaway slave.

"But if I had the soul of a free man, what then? Surely I would force my way back to Babylon, repay the people who had trusted me, bring happiness to my wife, who truly loved me, and bring peace and contentment to my parents. 'Thy debts are thine enemies, who have run thee out of Babylon,' Sira had said. Yes, it was so.

"Why had I refused to stand my ground like a man? Why had I permitted my wife to go back to her father? Then a strange thing happened. All the world seemed to be of a different color, as though I had been looking at it through a colored stone which had suddenly been removed. At last I saw the true values in life.

"Die in the desert! Not I! With a new vision, I saw the things that I must do. First, I would go back to Babylon and face every man to whom I owed an unpaid debt. I should tell them that after years of wandering and misfortune, I had come back to pay my debts as fast as the gods would permit. Next I should make a home for my wife and become a citizen of whom my parents should be proud.

"My debts were my enemies, but the men I owed were my friends, for they had trusted me and believed in me. I staggered weakly to my feet. What mattered hunger? What mattered thirst? They were but incidents on the road to Babylon.

"Within me surged the soul of a free man going back to conquer his enemies and reward his friends. I thrilled with the great resolve.

"The glazed eyes of my camels brightened at the new note in my husky voice. With great effort, after many

attempts, they gained their feet. With pitiful persever-
ance, they pushed on toward the north, where something
within me said we would find Babylon.

"We found water. We passed into a more fertile country where were grass and fruit. We found the trail to
Babylon, because the soul of a free man looks at life as
a series of problems to be solved and solves them, while
the soul of a slave whines, 'What can I do who am but a
slave?'

"How about thee, Tarkad? Dost thy empty stomach
make thy head exceedingly clear? Art ready to take the
road that leads back to self-respect? Canst thou see the
world in its true color? Hast thou the desire to pay thy
honest debts, however many they may be, and once again
be a man respected in Babylon?"

Moisture came to the eyes of the youth. He rose eagerly
to his knees. "Thou hast shown me a vision. Already I feel
the soul of a free man surge within me."

"But how fared you upon your return?" questioned an
interested listener.

"Where the determination is, the way can be found,"
Dabasir replied. "I now had the determination, so I set
out to find a way. First I visited every man to whom I was
indebted and begged his indulgence until I could earn
that with which to repay. Most of them met me gladly.
Several reviled me, but others offered to help me.

"One indeed did give me the very help I needed. It
was Mathon, the gold lender. Learning that I had been
a camel tender in Syria, he sent me to old Nebatur, the
camel trader, just commissioned by our good king to pur-

chase many herds of sound camels for the great expedition. With him, my knowledge of camels I put to good use. Gradually I was able to repay every copper and every piece of silver. Then at last I could hold up my head and feel that I was an honorable man among men."

Again Dabasir turned to his food. "Kauskor, thou snail," he called loudly, to be heard in the kitchen, "the food is cold. Bring me more meat fresh from the roasting. Bring thou also a very large portion for Tarkad, the son of my old friend, who is hungry and shall eat with me."

So ended the tale of Dabasir, the camel trader of old Babylon. He found his own soul when he realized a great truth, a truth that had been known and used by wise men long before his time. It has led men of all ages out of difficulties and into success, and it will continue to do so for those who have the wisdom to understand its magic power. It is for any man to use who hears these lines. Where the determination is, the way can be found.

## ❦ Dan ❧

In this chapter, Tarkad, the son of Azure, had borrowed copper and silver from all the people in Babylon, and he didn't have enough money to pay them back. He encountered another person, Dabasir, from whom he had borrowed two pieces of copper and one piece of silver a long time before.

Dabasir caught Tarkad and shared his story as a lesson. Dabasir had lived in Babylon with his wife. He realized that because he had such a great relationship with the shopkeepers of the town, they would let him take goods and services and pay later, but at some point he'd taken more than he could afford to pay back, given his earnings.

His life became miserable, and his wife returned to her father. Dabasir turned to a life of crime, robbing unarmed caravans, but in one of the robberies, he was caught and sold into slavery. While he was a slave, one of the wives of the owner asked Dabasir to take her to see her sick mother.

Dabasir mentioned that he wasn't always a slave; he used to be a free man. The wife, Sira, says, "How can you call yourself a free man when your weakness has brought you to this? If a man has in himself the soul of a slave, will he not become one no matter what his birth, even as water seeks its level? If a man has within him the soul of a free man, will he not become respected and honored in his own city in spite of his misfortune?"

This chapter covers many important concepts. First of all, it's saying that if you have gotten yourself into a lot of debt, your life will become miserable. Your wife might even leave you. Even if you don't turn to a life of crime and get sold into slavery, you're still not going to be a free person.

If you owe money to someone else, they own you, but—and this is important too—if you have the soul of a slave, you're going to get yourself into slavery no matter what. If you have the soul of a free man, you'll eventually get free in spite of your misfortune.

We've all seen this. You have two men, both of whom get laid off from their jobs. They both have to borrow a lot of money, and they find themselves deeply in debt, but one of them has the soul of a slave, meaning that he hasn't learned the Laws of Gold and is destined to make the same mistakes again and again.

The other has the soul of a free man. He understands the Laws of Gold, and even though he may be in an unfortunate situation, he's going to come out of it. Which one are you?

Here's a story from Tony Manganiello, author of *Great Credit for a Lifetime*:

I remember one Saturday morning waking up to the phone ringing. It was a debt collector. They tried to get me to pay them with the money I didn't have. Maybe you know the feeling. At that time in my life, collectors and creditors were calling regularly. I felt like a deli counter at the grocery store. I told them that they could try to get water from a stone, but they would have to take a number and get in line with the rest of the people I owed money to. When I hung up the phone, all I could think was, "How did I wind up here?"

The funny thing is, I didn't wake up one morning saying, "In one year I want to be breaking a sweat each time the phone rings or whenever I open the checkbook to pay my bills, and I want my financial situation to be so screwed up that hopelessness and discouragement are the most common emotions I experience."

"No one intentionally charts a course where the destination is embarrassment and despair. The question is, if quiet desperation and financial frustration aren't the intended destinations, why do so many people end up there? The answer: lack of knowledge.

Tony has the soul of a free man. He dug himself out of the hole, and as he puts it, "For me, things are different now, much different. The lessons I've leaned that made big changes in these areas for me are now at your fingertips." Those lessons can be found in Tony's excellent audio program "Great Credit for a Lifetime."

Here's another modern example. It's from financial guru Suze Orman. In her book, *The Laws of Money, the Lessons of Life*, she elaborates Five Laws of Money. They're slightly different from the Five Laws of Gold we learned in this program, but they're useful nonetheless.

The Five Laws of Money, according to Suze Orman are, number one: *truth creates money; lies destroy it.* This has to do with being honest in your dealings with money. Don't try to cheat people, don't steal, and don't pretend you have money that you don't.

Number two, *look at what you have, not what you had.* If you're not honest about what you have and are living based on what you had, you're only going to dig yourself deeper.

Number three: *do what is right for you before you do what is right for your money.* Suze says that the main point for this law is that money is a mirror. When you do what is right for you, it shows up in your money. When you don't, it also shows up in your money. It is necessary to put yourself first when it comes to making your financial decisions.

Number four, *invest in the known before the unknown.* This means you put money into saving for your retirement, for which you know you will need money, for paying down your debts, which you know you already have, and for paying for your expenses, which you know are already coming. Then you can focus on preparing for unexpected things.

Number five, always remember that *money has no power of its own*. Money is a servant to you. It is designed to go out and work for you, not the other way around.

Let's do an exercise. In this exercise, you're going to take a good, honest look at yourself. Have you had the soul of a slave, just getting yourself into debt again and again? Have you been lying to yourself and others about how much you spend, what you need, and when you need it?

Now don't worry if this is you. Most people are like this. They pay off their credit cards only to rack them up again. You aren't doomed. You just need knowledge.

Or maybe you really do have the soul of a free man, but life's circumstances have gotten you down and you're in a bad spot. Write down your thoughts about this in your journal.

Let's go on with the story. Sira eventually told Dabasir that he could run away with two camels and some food and water. He wandered the desert for nine days. He basically did what you just did; looked deep into his heart and asked if he had the soul of a slave or the soul of a free man.

He decided that he had the soul of a free man, went back to Babylon, got his wife back, and paid off all his debts. He was an inspiration to Tarkad, who had decided that he too had the soul of a free man and made a plan to repay all of his debts. It's not easy, but as it's said, where the determination is, the way can be found.

It's pretty easy to see how this applies to modern life. Most of us carry some kind of consumer debt. We have credit cards, bank loans, personal loans, and more. Some of us have the soul of a slave and are going to spend the rest of our lives indebted to someone else. You may not be a literal slave, but if you can't answer your phone or your door for fear that it's a debt collector, you're an emotional slave.

In "Transforming Debt into Wealth," John Cummuta talks about this concept of debt as slavery. He tells a story that shows how insane debt can be. It's a story about how the average person—we're calling him Mr. Jones—lives his life.

Mr. Jones goes off to college at age eighteen, armed with student loans to pay for it. While in college, he gets his first credit card and uses it to buy a computer, a high-def TV, an iPhone, and the other toys he sees his friends buying. By the time he's nineteen, still a teenager, he's making payments on an HDTV, a video game system, and a nice SUV to take himself from class to class.

He graduates from college, gets a modest job, and falls in love. He gets married and puts the wedding and honeymoon on his credit card. When he returns, they need a place to live, so they buy a small condo. The happy couple can't sleep on the bare floor, so they go to the local furniture store and buy furniture, appliances, plants, and lighting, all on the easy payment plan.

Soon they start having children and need kid things: a new minivan with a TV and GPS, of course vacations to Disneyland, and new school clothes every year from the local department store. Mr. Jones hasn't gotten that promotion yet at work, so they put it all on credit.

Then they move into a bigger home every seven years and trade cars every three and a half years. In eighteen years,

Mr. Jones's kids go off to college and start the cycle again, but the kids have to take out student loans just like Dad, because he's still paying off the debts from his college years.

Eventually, Mr. Jones turns sixty, and like many Americans, he can't figure out what went wrong. He worked his whole life, earned over a million dollars in his career, and has nothing to show for it. He's afraid that he and his bride will have to work until they die, because he sees no end to the bills and no hope of a retirement nest egg.

Mr. Jones simply did what he thought he should do, what everyone else around him was doing, but by following those around him who were simultaneously following him, Mr. Jones walked right into a prison of financial slavery. Unfortunately, that's what most people do.

Did you know that 96 percent of Americans fail to achieve true financial independence? True financial independence could be defined as having sufficient resources to live your life by your own means, not having to work, get money from charity, or rely on government subsidies.

Only about 4 percent of Americans enjoy that kind of financial freedom at retirement age. This means that most Americans, that 96 percent who fail to achieve financial independence, are not free. They're slaves from the day they become adults to the day they die.

Luckily, you have the power to release yourself from the chains of debt slavery. You don't have to steal camels and wander the desert for nine days, but you do have to make a commitment to become debt-free.

Whether you use the system outlined in "Transforming Debt into Wealth" or the one we outline here in the next chapter, or just do it yourself, the only way to become the richest man in Babylon is to get out of debt and stay out of debt.

## Babylon Builder

In this chapter, we learned all about debt and how owing more money than you can pay back is humiliating and stressful. You can lose everything that's important to you. But we also learned about the difference between the soul of a slave and the soul of a free person. You can get out of debt.

We learned about Suze Orman's Five Laws of Money. We talked about how insane it is to get buried in debt while trying to keep up with what society tells us we need to have. As for action steps, you did some soul searching. You hopefully made a commitment to become debt-free.

# TEN
# The Clay Tablets from Babylon

St. Swithin's College
Nottingham University
Newark-on-Trent, Nottingham
October 21, 1934

Professor Franklin Caldwell
Care of British Scientific Expedition
Hillah, Mesopotamia

My dear Professor:
The five clay tablets from your recent excavation in the ruins of Babylon arrived on the same boat with your letter. I have been fascinated no end, and have spent many pleasant hours translating their inscriptions. I should have answered your letter at once but delayed until I could complete the translations, which are attached. The tablets arrived without damage,

thanks to your careful use of preservatives and excellent packing.

You will be as astonished as we in the laboratory at the story they relate. One expects the dim and distant past to speak of romance and adventure, Arabian Nights sort of things, you know. When instead it discloses the problem of a person named Dabasir to pay off his debts, one realizes that conditions upon this old world have not changed as much in 5000 years as one might expect.

It's odd, you know, but these old inscriptions rather rag me, as the students say. Being a college professor, I am supposed to be a thinking human being possessing a working knowledge of most subjects. Yet here comes this old chap out of the dust-covered ruins of Babylon to offer a way I had never heard of to pay off my debts and at the same time acquire gold to jingle in my wallet.

Pleasant thought, I say, and interesting to prove whether it will work as well nowadays as it did in old Babylon. Mrs. Shrewsbury and myself are planning to try out his plan upon our own affairs, which could be much improved.

Wishing you the best of luck in your worthy undertaking and waiting eagerly another opportunity to assist.

I am yours sincerely,
Alfred H. Shrewsbury
Department of Archaeology

## TABLET 1

Now, when the moon becometh full, I, Dabasir, who am but recently returned from slavery in Syria, with the determination to pay my many just debts and become a man of means worthy of respect in my native city of Babylon, do here engrave upon the clay a permanent record of my affairs to guide and assist me in carrying through my high desires.

Under the wise advice of my good friend Mathon the gold lender, I am determined to follow an exact plan that he doth say will lead any honorable man out of debt into means and self-respect. This plan includeth three purposes which are my hope and desire.

First, the plan doth provide for my future prosperity. Therefore one-tenth of all I earn shall be set aside as my own to keep. For Mathon speaketh wisely when he saith, "That man who keepeth in his purse both gold and silver that he need not spend is good to his family and loyal to his king. The man who hath but a few coppers in his purse is indifferent to his family and indifferent to his king, but the man who hath naught in his purse is unkind to his family and is disloyal to his king, for his own heart is bitter. Therefore the man who wisheth to achieve must have coin that he may keep to jingle in his purse, that he have in his heart love for his family and loyalty to his king."

Second, the plan doth provide that I shall support and clothe my good wife, who hath returned to me with loyalty from the house of her father. For Mathon doth say that to take good care of a faithful wife putteth self-respect into the heart of a man and addeth strength and determination to his purposes.

Therefore, seven-tenths of all I earn shall be used to provide a home, clothes to wear, and food to eat, with a bit extra to spend, that our lives be not lacking in pleasure and enjoyment, but he doth further enjoin the greatest care that we spend not greater than seven-tenths of what I earn for these worthy purposes.

Herein lieth the success of the plan. I must live upon this portion and never use more nor buy what I may not pay for out of this portion.

## TABLET 2

Third, the plan doth provide that out of my earnings my debts shall be paid. Therefore, each time the moon is full, two-tenths of all I have earned shall be divided honorably and fairly among those who have trusted me and to whom I am indebted. Thus in due time will all my indebtedness be surely paid.

Therefore do I here engrave the name of every man to whom I am indebted and the honest amount of my debt.

Fahru, the cloth weaver: two silver, six copper.

Sinjar, the couchmaker: one silver.

Ahmar, my friend: three silver, one copper.

Zankar, my friend: four silver, seven copper.

Askamir, my friend: one silver, three copper.

Harinsir, the jewelmaker: six silver, two copper.

Diarbeker, my father's friend: four silver, one copper.

Alkahad, the house owner: fourteen silver.

Mathon, the gold lender: nine silver.

Birejik, the farmer: one silver, seven copper.

[From here on, disintegrated. Cannot be deciphered.]

## TABLET 3

To these creditors do I owe in total 119 pieces of silver and 141 pieces of copper. Because I did owe these sums and saw no way to repay, in my folly I did permit my wife to return to her father and did leave my native city and seek easy wealth elsewhere, only to find disaster and to see myself sold into the degradation of slavery.

Now that Mathon doth show me how I can repay my debts in small sums of my earnings do I realize the great extent of my folly in running away from the results of my extravagances. Therefore have I visited my creditors and explained to them that I have no resources with which to pay except my ability to earn, and that I intend to apply two-tenths of all I earn upon my indebtedness evenly and honestly. This much can I pay, but no more. Therefore, if they be patient, in time my obligations will be paid in full.

Ahmar, whom I thought my best friend, reviled me bitterly, and I left him in humiliation. Birejik, the farmer, pleaded that I pay him first as he did badly need help. Alkahad, the house owner, was indeed disagreeable and insisted that he would make me trouble unless I did soon settle in full with him.

All the rest willingly accepted my proposal. Therefore am I more determined than ever to carry through, being convinced that it is easier to pay one's just debts than to avoid them. Even though I cannot meet the needs and demands of a few of my creditors, I will deal impartially with all.

## TABLET 4

Again the moon shines full. I have worked hard with a free mind. My good wife hath supported my intentions to pay my creditors. Because of our wise determination, I have earned during the past moon, buying camels of sound wind and good legs, for Nebatur, the sum of nineteen pieces of silver.

This I have divided according to the plan. One-tenth have I set aside to keep as my own, seven-tenths have I divided with my good wife to pay for our living. Two-tenths have I divided among my creditors as evenly as could be done in coppers.

I did not see Ahmar but left it with his wife. Birejik was so pleased he would kiss my hand. Old Alkahad alone was grouchy and said I must pay faster, to which I replied that if I were permitted to be well fed and not worried, that alone would enable me to pay faster. All the others thanked me and spoke well of my efforts.

Therefore, at the end of one moon, my indebtedness is reduced by almost four pieces of silver, and I possess almost two pieces of silver besides, upon which no man hath claim. My heart is lighter than it hath been for a long time.

Again the moon shines full. I have worked hard, but with poor success. Few camels have I been able to buy. Only eleven pieces of silver have I earned. Nevertheless, my good wife and I have stood by the plan, even though we have bought no new raiment and eaten little but herbs.

Again I paid ourselves one-tenth of the eleven pieces, while we lived upon seven-tenths. I was surprised when Ahmar commended my payment, even though small. So did Birejik. Alkahad flew into a rage, but when told to give back his portion if he did not wish it, he became reconciled. The others, as before, were content.

Again the moon shines full, and I am greatly rejoiced. I intercepted a fine herd of camels and bought many sound ones; therefore my earnings were forty-two pieces of silver. This moon my wife and myself have bought much-needed sandals and raiment. Also, we have dined well on meat and fowl.

More than eight pieces of silver we have paid to our creditors. Even Alkahad did not protest. Great is the plan, for it leadeth us out of debt and giveth us wealth which is ours to keep.

Three times the moon had been full since I last carved upon this clay. Each time I paid to myself one-tenth of all I earned. Each time my good wife and I have lived upon seven-tenths, even though at times it was difficult. Each time have I paid to my creditors two-tenths.

In my purse I now have twenty-one pieces of silver that are mine. It maketh my head to stand straight upon my shoulders and maketh me proud to walk among my friends. My wife keepeth well our home and is becomingly gowned. We are happy to live together.

The plan is of untold value. Hath it not made an honorable man of an ex-slave?

## TABLET 5

Again the moon shines full, and I remember that it is long since I carved upon the clay. Twelve moons in truth have come and gone, but this day I will not neglect my record, because upon this day I have paid the last of my debts. This is the day upon which my good wife and my thankful self celebrate with great feasting that our determination hath been achieved.

Many things occurred upon my final visit to my creditors that I shall long remember. Ahmar begged my forgiveness for his unkind words and said that I was one of all others he most desired for a friend. Old Alkahad is not so bad after all, for he said, "Thou wert once a piece of soft clay to be pressed and molded by any hand that touched thee, but now thou art a piece of bronze capable of holding an edge. If thou needest silver or gold at any time, come to me."

Nor is he the only one who holdeth me in high regard. Many others speak deferentially to me. My good wife looketh upon me with a light in her eyes that doth make a man have confidence in himself. Yet it is the plan that hath made my success. It hath enabled me to pay all my debts and to jingle both gold and silver in my purse.

I do commend it to all who wish to get ahead. For truly if it will enable an ex-slave to pay his debts and have gold in his purse, will it not aid any man to find independence? Nor am I myself finished with it, for I am convinced that if I follow it further it will make me rich among men.

St. Swithin's College
Nottingham University
Newark-on-Trent
Nottingham
November 7, 1936

Professor Franklin Caldwell
Care of British Scientific Expedition
Hillah, Mesopotamia

My dear Professor:

If, in your further digging into those ruins of Babylon, you encounter the ghost of a former resident, an old camel trader named Dabasir, do me a favor. Tell him that his scribbling upon those clay tablets, so long ago, has earned for him the lifelong gratitude of a couple of college folks back here in England.

You will possibly remember my writing a year ago that Mrs. Shrewsbury and myself intended to try his plan for getting out of debt and at the same time having gold to jingle. You may have guessed, even though we tried to keep it from our friends, our desperate straits.

We were frightfully humiliated for years by a lot of old debts and worried sick for fear some of the trades-people might start a scandal that would force me out of the college. We paid and paid every shilling we could squeeze out of income, but it was hardly enough to hold things even. Besides, we were forced to do all our buying where we could get further credit, regard-less of higher costs.

It developed into one of those vicious circles that grow worse instead of better. Our struggles were getting hopeless. We could not move to less costly rooms, because we owed the landlord. There did not appear to be anything we could do to improve our situation.

Then, here comes your acquaintance, the old camel trader from Babylon, with a plan to do just what we wished to accomplish. He jolly well stirred us up to follow his system. We made a list of all our debts, and I took it around and showed it to everyone we owed. I explained how it was simply impossible for me to ever pay them the way things were going along. They could readily see this themselves from the figures.

Then I explained that the only way I saw to pay in full was to set aside 20 percent of my income each month to be divided pro rata, which would pay them in full in a little over two years. That, in the meantime, we would go on a cash basis and give them the further benefit of our cash purchases.

They were really quite decent. Our greengrocer, a wise old chap, put it in a way that helped to bring around the rest. "If you pay for all you buy and then pay some on what you owe, that is better than you have done, for ye ain't paid down the account none in three years."

Finally I secured all their names to an agreement binding them not to molest us as long as the 20 percent of income was paid regularly. Then we began scheming on how to live upon 70 percent. We were determined to keep that extra 10 percent to jingle. The thought of silver and possibly gold was most alluring.

It was like having an adventure to make the change. We enjoyed figuring this way and that, to live comfortably upon that remaining 70 percent. We started with rent and managed to secure a fair reduction. Next we put our favorite brands of tea and such under suspicion and were agreeably surprised how often we could purchase superior qualities at less cost.

It is too long a story for a letter, but anyhow it did not prove difficult. We managed, and right cheerfully at that. What a relief it proved to have our affairs in such a shape we were no longer persecuted by past due accounts. I must not neglect, however, to tell you about that extra 10 percent we were supposed to jingle.

Well, we did jingle it for some time. Now don't laugh too soon. You see, that is the sporty part. It is the real fun, to start accumulating money that you do not want to spend. There is more pleasure in running up such a surplus than there could be in spending it.

After we had jingled to our hearts' content, we found a more profitable use for it. We took up an investment upon which we could pay that 10 percent each month. This is proving to be the most satisfying part of our regeneration. It is the first thing we pay out of my check.

There is a most gratifying sense of security to know our investment is growing steadily. By the time my teaching days are over it should be a snug sum, large enough so the income will take care of us from then on. All this out of my same old check.

Difficult to believe, yet absolutely true. All our debts being gradually paid, and at the same time our investment increasing. Besides, we get along, financially, even better than before. Who would believe there could be such a difference in results between following a financial plan and just drifting along?

At the end of the next year, when all our old bills shall have been paid, we will have more to pay upon our investment, besides some extra for travel. We are determined never again to permit our living expenses to exceed 70 percent of our income. Now you can understand why we would like to extend our personal thanks to that old chap whose plan saved us from our hell on earth.

He knew. He had been through it all. He wanted others to benefit from his own bitter experiences. That is why he spent tedious hours carving his message upon the clay. He had a real message for fellow sufferers, a message so important that after 5,000 years it has risen out of the ruins of Babylon, just as true and just as vital as the day it was buried.

Yours sincerely,

Alfred H. Shrewsbury

Department of Archaeology

# ⋖ Dan ⋗

Although *The Richest Man in Babylon* was created as a compilation of a series of pamphlets, what we learned in this chapter is that the lessons contained within the book can apply to modern times. (Of course, by now 1934 isn't modern, but when the book came out originally, it was the current time.)

The story is told through a series of memos from Alfred Shrewsbury to Franklin Caldwell, an archeologist who discovered five clay tablets in 1934 that were left from Babylonian times. They were written by Dabasir, the guy who got sold into slavery for robbing a caravan, and they detail his plan to get out of debt.

Let's go through the tablets one by one and apply the ideas to your debt-reduction plan. In the first tablet, Dabasir talks about his commitment to get out of debt. He got some wise advice from Mathon, the gold lender, and devised a three-part plan.

First, he's keeping one-tenth of what he earns for his future prosperity. You're doing that now too. Second, Dabasir is so happy that his wife agreed to come back that he realized he needs to focus on supporting his family. Dabasir commits to spending seven-tenths of his income on his regular expenses. We'll talk about this more in a few minutes.

Then, in Tablet 2, Dabasir says that he's going to spend two-tenths of his income paying down his debts. His lists his creditors and how much owes them.

In Tablet 3, Dabasir shares how horrible he feels that it got this bad and goes to make a personal visit to each of his creditors to share the plan for repayment. Some were disagreeable about it, but they accepted the repayment plan. He comments that even though he can't meet the needs of everyone, he's going to deal impartially with them all.

In the fourth tablet, Dabasir gives us an update and says that he's making good progress on his debt reduction. One creditor was still being grouchy about it, but Dabasir continued with his plan. He shares that he's not really been able to afford a lot of new things, but that they stand committed to the plan.

Finally, in the fifth and last tablet, Dabasir has paid the last of his debts. It's been a year, and he's debt-free. Even cranky old Alkahad came around and begged Dabasir for his forgiveness for the way he'd acted.

The rest of the chapter is from Alfred Shrewsbury as he relates how his debt reduction process went.

We can learn a lot from Dabasir. It wasn't easy for him to admit that he'd been wrong. It took a lot of self-sacrifice, and he had to put his ego aside.

Let's apply this to your situation. We're assuming here that you're one of the millions of people who have outstanding debt. First, you need to make a commitment that you're going to do whatever it takes to get out of debt. Surely you've seen the need for it by now. Also, there is some debate among modern experts about whether you should save money along with debt reduction, or just focus all of our resources on debt reduction. Dabasir did both.

So you're saving 10 percent of your income off the top. Then you take 70 percent of your income, and you use that to pay your monthly living expenses. I can hear some of you now, "But, Dan, I can't live on only 70 percent of my income. That's not enough."

Well, this is where you're going to have to get tough. Remember that exercise we did early where you logged your expenses? If you can't live on 70 percent of your income, then you're going to need to cut back. Slash the cable bills. Lower your cell-phone minutes. Stop eating out as much. Don't buy new clothes. Stop going to the movies.

What ever you need to do, do it. This is your life and your future we're talking about here. It's not forever; it's just until you get your debts paid off.

Next, you need to make a list of everyone you owe money to. This may be the same list as your liabilities list, or you may have more, but make a list of everyone you owe money to and how much you owe them, and decide whom you're going to pay first and how much. Basically, you want to pay off the highest-interest debts first. Remember, you're dedicating 20 percent of your income to this. With 20 percent, these debts are going to go fast.

Now comes the uncomfortable part. You have to contact all of your creditors and tell them your plan. Like Alkahad, not all of them are going to be agreeable, but it doesn't matter. This is your plan. Don't let your creditors threaten you, guilt you, or push you into something else. Like Suze Orman says, you have to do what is right for you first. You're going to do the right thing, and you're never going to get into this situation again.

Next, it's just a matter of implementing your plan. It's a good idea to recalculate your debts every once in a while. It'll make you feel better. Pretty soon your debts will be paid off, and that 20 percent of your income can go to investing, to buying some of the fun stuff that you put off while you were working your plan, or to saving for something for the future.

Now you know that I'm not going to let you off the hook by just talking and not having you apply what we're learning, so your exercise for this session is to make that list of debts and make those phone calls. The sooner you get it over with, the better you'll feel.

Are you ready? Go do it.

Did you do it? I hope you did. This is a difficult but critically important step, and if you did it, how do you feel? About ten pounds lighter, I'll bet.

### Babylon Builder

In this chapter, we learned a five-step plan for getting out of debt, and your exercise is to follow it.

# ELEVEN
# The Luckiest Man
# in Babylon

At the head of his caravan proudly rode Sharru Nada, the merchant prince of Babylon. He liked fine cloth and wore rich and becoming robes. He liked fine animals and sat easily upon his spirited Arabian stallion. To look at him, one would hardly have guessed his advanced years. Certainly they would not have suspected that he was inwardly troubled.

The journey from Damascus is long and the hardships of the desert many. These he minded not. The Arab tribes are fierce and eager to loot rich caravans. These he feared not, for his many fleet-mounted guards were a safe protection.

About the youth at his side, whom he was bringing from Damascus, was he disturbed. This was Hadan Gula, the grandson of his partner of other years, Arad Gula, to whom he felt he owed a debt of gratitude which could never be repaid. He would like to do something for this grandson, but the more he considered this, the more difficult it seemed because of the youth himself.

Eyeing the young man's rings and earrings, he thought to himself, "He thinks jewels are for men. Still he has his grandfather's strong face, but his grandfather wore no such gaudy robes. Yet I sought him to come, hoping I might help him get a start for himself and get away from the wreck his father has made of their inheritance."

Hadan Gula broke in upon his thoughts. "Why dost thou work so hard, riding always with thy caravan upon its long journeys? Dost thou never take time to enjoy life?"

Sharru Nada smiled. "To enjoy life?" he repeated. "What wouldst thou do to enjoy life if thou wert Sharru Nada?"

"If I had wealth equal to thine, I would live like a prince. Never across the hot desert would I ride. I would spend the shekels as fast as they came to my purse. I would wear the richest of robes and the rarest of jewels. That would be a life to my liking, a life worth living." Both men laughed.

"Thy grandfather wore no jewels." Sharru Nada spoke before he thought, then continued jokingly, "Wouldst thou leave no time for work?"

"Work was made for slaves," Hadan Gula responded. Sharru Nada bit his lip but made no reply, riding in silence until the trail led them to the slope. Here he reined his mount and pointing to the green valley far away. "See, there is the valley. Look far down and thou canst faintly see the walls of Babylon. The tower is the Temple of Bel. If thine eyes are sharp thou mayest even see the smoke from the eternal fire upon its crest."

"So that is Babylon? Always have I longed to see the wealthiest city in all the world," Hadan Gula commented. "Babylon, where my grandfather started his fortune. Would he were still alive! We would not be so sorely pressed."

"Why wish his spirit to linger on earth beyond its allotted time? Thou and thy father can well carry on his good work."

"Alas, of us, neither has his gift. Father and myself know not his secret for attracting the golden shekels."

Sharru Nada did not reply but gave rein to his mount and rode thoughtfully down the trail to the valley. Behind them followed the caravan in a cloud of reddish dust. Some time later they reached the king's highway and turned south through the irrigated farms.

Three old men plowing a field caught Sharru Nada's attention. They seemed strangely familiar. How ridiculous! One does not pass a field after forty years and find the same men plowing there. Yet something within him said they were the same. One, with an uncertain grip, held the plow. The others laboriously plodded beside the oxen, ineffectually beating them with their barrel staves to keep them pulling.

Forty years ago he had envied these men. How gladly he would have exchanged places, but what a difference now! With pride he looked back at his trailing caravan, well-chosen camels and donkeys, loaded high with valuable goods from Damascus. All this was but one of his possessions. He pointed to the plowers, saying, "Still plowing the same field where they were forty years ago."

"They look it, but why thinkest thou they are the same?

"I saw them there," Sharru Nada replied. Recollections were racing rapidly through his mind. Why could he not bury the past and live in the present? Then he saw, as in a picture, the smiling face of Arad Gula. The barrier between himself and the cynical youth beside him dissolved, but how could he help such a superior youth with his spendthrift ideas and bejeweled hands?

Work he could offer in plenty to willing workers, but naught for men who considered themselves too good for work. Yet he owed it to Arad Gula to do something—not a half-hearted attempt. He and Arad Gula had never done things that way. They were not that sort of men.

A plan came almost in a flash. There were objections. He must consider his own family and his own standing. It would be cruel. It would hurt. Being a man of quick decisions, he waived objections and decided to act.

"Wouldst thou be interested in hearing how thy worthy grandfather and myself joined in the partnership which proved so profitable?" he questioned.

"Why not just tell me how thou madest the golden shekels? That is all I need to know," the young man parried.

Sharru Nada ignored the reply and continued, "We start with those men plowing. I was no older than thou. As the column of men in which I marched approached, good old Megiddo the farmer scoffed at the slipshod way in which they plowed. Megiddo was chained next to me. 'Look at the lazy fellows,' he protested, 'the plow holder makes no effort to plow deep, nor do the beaters keep the oxen in the furrow. How can they expect to raise a good crop with poor plowing?'

"Didst thou say Megiddo was chained to thee?" Hadan Gula asked in surprise.

"Yes, with bronze collars about our necks and a length of heavy chain between us. Next to him was Zabado, the sheep thief. I had known him in Harroun. At the end was a man we called Pirate because he told us not his name. We judged him as a sailor, as he had entwined serpents tattooed upon his chest in sailor fashion. The column was made up thus so the men could walk in fours."

"Thou wert chained as a slave?" Hadan Gula asked incredulously.

"Did not thy grandfather tell thee I was once a slave?"

"He often spoke of thee but never hinted of this."

"He was a man thou couldst trust with innermost secrets. Thou too are a man I may trust, am I not right?"

Sharru Nada looked him squarely in the eye. "Thou mayest rely upon my silence, but I am amazed. Tell me: how didst thou come to be a slave?"

Sharru Nada shrugged his shoulders. "Any man may find himself a slave. It was a gaming house and barley beer that brought me disaster. I was the victim of my brother's indiscretions. In a brawl he killed his friend. I was bonded to the widow by my father, desperate to keep my brother from being prosecuted under the law. When my father could not raise the silver to free me, she in anger sold me to the slave dealer."

"What a shame and injustice," Hadan Gula protested. "But tell me: how didst thou regain freedom?"

"We shall come to that, but not yet. Let us continue my tale. As we passed, the plowers jeered us. One did doff his ragged hat and bow low, calling out, 'Welcome to Babylon, guests of the king. He waits for thee on the city walls, where the banquet is spread, mud bricks and onion soup.' With that they laughed uproariously.

"Pirate flew into a rage and cursed them roundly.

"'What do those men mean by the king awaiting us on the walls?' I asked him.

"'To the city walls ye march to carry bricks until the back breaks. Maybe they beat thee to death before it breaks. They won't beat me. I'll kill 'em.'

"Then Megiddo spoke up. 'It doesn't make sense to me to talk of masters beating willing, hard-working slaves to death. Masters like good slaves and treat them well.'

"'Who wants to work hard?' commented Zabado. 'Those plowers are wise fellows. They're not breaking their backs, just letting on as if they be.'

"'Thou canst not get ahead by shirking,' Megiddo protested. If thou plow a hectare, that's a good day's work and any master knows it, but when thou plowest only a half, that's shirking. I don't shirk. I like to work, and I like to do good work, for work is the best friend I've ever known. It has brought me all the good things I've had, my farm and cows and crops, everything.'

"'Yea, and where be these things now?' scoffed Zabado. 'I figure it pays better to be smart and get by without working. You watch Zabado. If we're sold to the walls, he'll be carrying the water bag or some easy job when thou, who like to work, wilt be breaking thy back carrying bricks.' He laughed his silly laugh.

"Terror gripped me that night. I could not sleep. I crowded close to the guard rope, and when the others slept, I attracted the attention of Godoso, who was doing the first guard watch. He was one of those brigand Arabs, the sort of rogue who, if he robbed thee of thy purse, would think he must also cut thy throat.

"'Tell me, Godoso,' I whispered, 'when we get to Babylon will we be sold to the walls?'

"'Why want to know?' he questioned cautiously.

"'Canst thou not understand?' I pleaded. 'I am young. I want to live. I don't want to be worked or beaten to death on the walls. Is there any chance for me to get a good master?'

"He whispered back, 'I tell something. Thou good fellow, give Godoso no trouble. Most times we go first to slave market. Listen now. When buyers come, tell 'em you good worker, like to work hard for good master. Make 'em want to buy. You not make 'em buy, next day you carry brick. Mighty hard work.'

"After he walked away, I lay in the warm sand, looking up at the stars and thinking about work. What Megiddo had said about it being his best friend made me wonder if it would be my best friend. Certainly it would be if it helped me out of this.

"When Megiddo awoke, I whispered my good news to him. It was our one ray of hope as we marched toward Babylon. Late in the afternoon we approached the walls and could see the lines of men, like black ants, climbing up and down the steep diagonal paths. As we drew closer, we were amazed at the thousands of men working; some were digging in the moat, others mixed the dirt into mud bricks. The greatest number were carrying the bricks in large baskets up those steep trails to the masons."*

"Overseers cursed the laggards and cracked bullock whips over the backs of those who failed to keep in line. Poor, worn-out fellows were seen to stagger and fall beneath their heavy baskets, unable to rise again. If the lash failed to bring them to their feet, they were pushed to the side of the paths and left writhing in agony. Soon they would be dragged down to join other craven bodies beside the roadway to await unsanctified graves.

"As I beheld the ghastly sight, I shuddered. So this was what awaited my father's son if he failed at the slave market. Godoso had been right. We were taken through the gates of the city to the slave prison and next morning marched to the pens in the market. Here the rest of the men huddled in fear, and only the whips of our guard could keep them moving so the buyers could examine them. Megiddo and myself eagerly talked to every man who permitted us to address him.

---

* The famous works of ancient Babylon, its walls, temples, Hanging Gardens and great canals, were built by slave labor, mainly prisoners of war, which explains the inhuman treatment they received. This force of workmen also included many citizens of Babylon and its provinces who had been sold into slavery because of crimes or financial troubles. It was a common custom for men to put themselves, their wives, or their children up as a bond to guarantee payment of loans, legal judgments, or other obligations. In case of default, those so bonded were sold into slavery.

"The slave dealer brought soldiers from the King's Guard, who shackled Pirate and brutally beat him when he protested. As they led him away, I felt sorry for him.

"Megiddo felt that we would soon part. When no buyers were near, he talked to me earnestly to impress upon me how valuable work would be to me in the future. 'Some men hate it. They make it their enemy. Better to treat it like a friend, make thyself like it. Don't mind because it is hard. If thou thinkest about what a good house thou buildest, then who cares if the beams are heavy and it is far from the well to carry the water for the plaster? Promise me, boy, if thou gettest a master, work for him as hard as thou canst. If he does not appreciate all thou dost, never mind. Remember, work, well done, does good to the man who does it. It makes him a better man.'

"He stopped as a burly farmer came to the enclosure and looked at us critically. Megiddo asked about his farm and crops, soon convincing him that he would be a valuable man. After violent bargaining with the slave dealer, the farmer drew a fat purse from beneath his robe, and soon Megiddo had followed his new master out of sight.

"A few other men were sold during the morning. At noon, Godoso confided to me that the dealer was disgusted and would not stay over another night but would take all who remained at sundown to the king's buyer. I was becoming desperate when a fat, good-natured man walked up to the wall and inquired if there was a baker among us.

"I approached him saying, 'Why should a good baker like thyself seek another baker of inferior ways? Would it not be easier to teach a willing man like myself thy skilled ways? Look at me, I am young, strong, and like to work. Give me a chance, and I will do my best to earn gold and silver for thy purse.'

"He was impressed by my willingness and began bargaining with the dealer, who had never noticed me since he had bought me, but now waxed eloquent on my abilities, good health, and good disposition. I felt like a fat ox being sold to a butcher. At last, much to my joy, the deal was closed. I followed my new master away, thinking I was the luckiest man in Babylon.

"My new home was much to my liking. Nana-naid, my master, taught me how to grind the barley in the stone bowl that stood in the courtyard, how to build the fire in the oven, and then how to grind very fine the sesame flour for the honey cakes. I had a couch in the shed where his grain was stored. The old slave housekeeper, Swasti, fed me well and was pleased at the way I helped her with the heavy tasks.

"Here was the chance I had longed for to make myself valuable to my master and, I hoped, to find a way to earn my freedom. I asked Nana-naid to show me how to knead the bread and to bake. This he did, much pleased at my willingness. Later, when I could do this well, I asked him to show me how to make the honey cakes, and soon I was doing all the baking. My master was glad to be idle, but Swasti shook her head in disapproval, 'No work to do is bad for any man.'

"I felt it was time for me to think of a way by which I might start to earn coins to buy my freedom. As the baking was finished at noon, I thought Nana-naid would approve if I found profitable employment for the afternoons and might share my earnings with me. Then the thought came to me, why not bake more of the honey cakes and peddle them to hungry men upon the streets of the city?

"I presented my plan to Nana-naid this way. 'If I can use my afternoons after the baking is finished to earn for thee coins, would it be only fair for thee to share my earnings with me, that I might have money of my own to spend for those things which every man desires and needs?'

"'Fair enough, fair enough,' he admitted. When I told him of my plan to peddle our honey cakes, he was well pleased. 'Here is what we will do,' he suggested. 'Thou sellest them at two for a penny, then half of the pennies will be mine to pay for the flour and the honey and the wood to bake them. Of the rest, I shall take half and thou shall keep half.'

"I was much pleased by his generous offer that I might keep for myself one-fourth of my sales. That night I worked late to make a tray upon which to display them. Nana-naid gave me one of his worn robes that I might look well, and Swasti helped me patch it and wash it clean.

"The next day I baked an extra supply of honey cakes. They looked brown and tempting upon the tray as I went along the street, loudly calling my wares. At first no one seemed interested, and I became discouraged. I kept on and later in the afternoon as men became hungry, the cakes began to sell, and soon my tray was empty. Nana-naid was well pleased with my success and gladly paid me my share. I was delighted to own pennies. Megiddo had been right when he said a master appreciated good work from his slaves.

"That night I was so excited over my success I could hardly sleep, and tried to figure how much I could earn in a year and how many years would be required to buy my freedom.

"As I went forth with my tray of cakes every day, I soon found regular customers. One of these was none other than thy grandfather, Arad Gula. He was a rug merchant and sold to the housewives, going from one end of the city the other, accompanied by a donkey loaded high with rugs and a black slave to tend it. He would buy two cakes for himself and two for his slave, always tarrying to talk with me while they ate them.

"Thy grandfather said something to me one day that I shall always remember. 'I like thy cakes, boy, but better still I like the fine enterprise with which thou offerest them. Such spirit can carry thee far on the road to success.'

"But how canst thou understand, Hadan Gula, what such words of encouragement could mean to a slave boy, lonesome in a great city, struggling with all he had in him to find a way out of his humiliation? As the months went by, I continued to add pennies to my purse. It began to have a comforting weight upon my belt. Work was proving to be my best friend, just as Megiddo had said.

"I was happy, but Swasti was worried. 'Thy master, I fear to have him spend so much time at the gaming houses.'

"I was overjoyed one day to meet my friend Megiddo upon the street. He was leading three donkeys loaded with vegetables to the market. 'I am doing mighty well,' he said. 'My master does appreciate my good work, for now I am a foreman. See, he does trust the marketing to me, and also he is sending for my family. Work is helping me to recover from my great trouble. Someday it will help me to buy my freedom and once more own a farm of my own.'

"Time went on, and Nana-naid became more and more anxious for me to return from selling. He would be waiting when I returned and would eagerly count and divide our money. He would also urge me to seek further markets and increase my sales.

"Often I went outside the city gates to solicit the overseers of the slaves building the walls. I hated to return to the disagreeable sights but found the overseers liberal buyers. One day, I was surprised to see Zabado waiting in line to fill his basket with bricks. He was gaunt and bent, and his back was covered with welts and sores from the whips of the overseers. I was sorry for him and handed him a cake, which he crushed into his mouth like a hungry animal. Seeing the greedy look in his eyes, I ran before he could grab my tray.

"'Why dost thou work so hard?' Arad Gula said to me one day—almost the same question thou askedst of me today. Dost thou remember? I told him what Megiddo had said about work and how it was proving to be my best friend. I showed him with pride my wallet of pennies and explained how I was saving them to buy my freedom.

"'When thou art free, what wilt thou do?' he inquired.

"'Then,' I answered, 'I intend to become a merchant.'

"At that, he confided in me something I had never suspected. 'Thou knowest not that I also am a slave. I am in partnership with my master.'

"Stop," demanded Hadan Gula. "I will not listen to lies defaming my grandfather. He was no slave." His eyes blazed in anger.

Sharru Nada remained calm. "I honor him for rising above his misfortune and becoming a leading citizen of Damascus. Art thou, his grandson, cast of the same mold? Art thou man enough to face true facts, or dost thou prefer to live under false illusions?"

Hadan Gula straightened in his saddle. In a voice suppressed with deep emotion he replied, "My grandfather was beloved by all. Countless were his good deeds. When the famine came did not his gold buy grain in Egypt, and did not his caravan bring it to Damascus and distribute it to the people so none would starve? Now thou sayest he was but a despised slave in Babylon."

Sharru Nada replied. "Had he remained a slave in Babylon, then he might well have been despised, but when, through his own efforts, he became a great man in Damascus, the gods indeed condoned his misfortunes and honored him with their respect. After telling me that he was a slave," Sharru Nada continued, "he explained how anxious he had been to earn his freedom.

"Now that he had enough money to buy this, he was much disturbed as to what he should do. He was no longer making good sales and feared to leave the support of his master.

"I protested his indecision. 'Cling no longer to thy master. Get once again the feeling of being a free man. Act like a free man and succeed like one. Decide what thou desirest to accomplish, and then work will aid thee to achieve it.' He went on his way saying he was glad I had shamed him for his cowardice.*

"One day I went outside the gates again, and was surprised to find a great crowd gathering there. When I asked a man for an explanation he replied, 'Hast thou not heard? An escaped slave who murdered one of the king's guards has been brought to justice and will this day be flogged to death for his crime. Even the king himself is to be here.'

"So dense was the crowd about the flogging post, I feared to go near lest my tray of honey cakes be upset. Therefore I climbed up the unfinished wall to see over the heads of the people. I was fortunate in having a view of Nebuchadnezzar himself as he rode by in his golden chariot. Never had I beheld such grandeur, such robes, and hangings of gold cloth and velvet.

"I could not see the flogging, though I could hear the shrieks of the poor slave. I wandered how one so noble as our handsome king could endure to see such suffering, yet when I saw he was laughing and joking with his

---

* Slave customs in ancient Babylon, though they may seem inconsistent to us, were strictly regulated by law. For example, a slave could own property of any kind, even other slaves upon which his master had no claim. Slaves intermarried freely with nonslaves. Children of free mothers were free. Most of the city merchants were slaves. Many of these were in partnership with their masters and wealthy in their own right.

nobles, I knew he was cruel and understood why such inhuman tasks were demanded of the slaves building the walls.

"After the slave was dead, his body was hung upon a pole by a rope attached to his leg so all might see. As the crowd began to thin, I went close. On the hairy chest, I saw tattooed two entwined serpents. It was Pirate.

"The next time I met Arad Gula, he was a changed man. Full of enthusiasm he greeted me, 'Behold, the slave thou knewest is now a free man. There was magic in thy words. Already my sales and my profits are increasing. My wife is overjoyed. She was a free woman, the niece of my master. She much desires that we move to a strange city where no man shall know I was once a slave. Thus our children shall be above reproach for their father's misfortune. Work has become my best helper. It has enabled me to recapture my confidence and my skill to sell.'

"I was overjoyed that I had been able even in a small way, to repay him for the encouragement he had given me. One evening Swasti came to me in deep distress. 'Thy master is in trouble. I fear for him. Some months ago he lost much at the gaming tables. He pays not the farmer for his grain nor his honey. He pays not the moneylender. They are angry and threaten him.'

"'Why should we worry over his folly? We are not his keepers,' I replied thoughtlessly.

"'Foolish youth, thou understandest not. To the moneylender did he give thy title to secure a loan. Under the law he can claim thee and sell thee. I know not what to do. He is a good master. Why, oh why, should such trouble come upon him?'

"Nor were Swasti's fears groundless. While I was doing the baking next morning, the moneylender returned with a man he called Sasi. This man looked me over and said I would do. The moneylender waited not for my master to return but told Swasti to tell him he had taken me.

"With only the robe on my back and the purse of pennies hanging safely from my belt, I was hurried away from the unfinished baking. I was whirled away from my dearest hopes as the hurricane snatches the tree from the forest and casts it into the surging sea. Again a gaming house and barley beer had caused me disaster.

"Sasi was a blunt, gruff man. As he led me across the city, I told him of the good work I had been doing for Nana-naid and said I hoped to do good work for him. His reply offered no encouragement. 'I like not this work. My master likes it not. The king has told him to send me to build a section of the Grand Canal. Master tells Sasi to buy more slaves, work hard, and finish quick. Bah. How can any man finish a big job quick?'

"Picture a desert with not a tree, just low shrubs, and a sun burning with such fury the water in our barrels became so hot we could scarcely drink it. Then picture rows of men, going down into the deep excavation and lugging heavy baskets of dirt up soft, dusty trails from daylight until dark. Picture food served in open troughs, from which we helped ourselves like swine.

"We had no tents, no straw for beds. That was the situation in which I found myself. I buried my wallet in a marked spot, wondering if I would ever dig it up again. At first I worked with goodwill, but as the months dragged on, I felt my spirit breaking.

"Then the heat fever took hold of my weary body. I lost my appetite and could scarcely eat the mutton and vegetables. At night I would toss in unhappy wakefulness. In my misery, I wondered if Zabado had not the best plan, to shirk and keep his back from being broken in work. Then I recalled my last sight of him and knew his plan was not good.

"I thought of Pirate with his bitterness and wondered if it might be just as well to fight and kill. The memory of his bleeding body reminded me that his plan was also useless. Then I remembered my last sight of Megiddo. His hands were deeply calloused from hard work, but his heart was light and there was happiness on his face. His was the best plan.

"Yet I was just as willing to work as Megiddo; he could not have worked harder than I. Why did not my work bring me happiness and success? Was it work that brought Megiddo happiness, or was happiness and success merely in the laps of the gods? Was I to work the rest of my life without gaining my desires, without happiness and success?

"All of these questions were jumbled in my mind, and I had not an answer. Indeed, I was sorely confused. Several days later, when it seemed that I was at the end of my endurance and my questions still unanswered, Sasi sent for me. A messenger had come from my master to take me back to Babylon. I dug up my precious wallet, wrapped myself in the tattered remnants of my robe, and was on my way.

"As we rode, the same thoughts of a hurricane whirling me hither and thither kept racing through my feverish brain. I seemed to be living the weird words of a chant from my native town of Harroun:

> *Besetting a man like a whirlwind,*
> *Driving him like a storm,*
> *Whose course no one can follow,*
> *Whose destiny no one can foretell.*

"Was I destined to be ever thus punished for I knew not what? What new miseries and disappointments awaited me? When we rode to the courtyard of my master's house, imagine my surprise when I saw Arad Gula awaiting me. He helped me down and hugged me like a long-lost brother.

"As we went our way, I would have followed him as a slave should follow his master, but he would not permit me. He put his arm about me, saying, 'I hunted everywhere for thee. When I had almost given up hope, I did meet Swasti, who told me of the moneylender, who directed me to thy noble owner. A hard bargain he did drive and made me pay an outrageous price, but thou art worth it. Thy philosophy and thy enterprise have been my inspiration to this new success.'

"'Megiddo's philosophy, not mine,' I interrupted.

"'Megiddo's and thine. Thanks to thee both, we are going to Damascus, and I need thee for my partner. See,' he exclaimed, 'in one moment thou wilt be a free man.' So saying, he drew from beneath his robe the clay tablet carrying my title. This he raised above his head and hurled it to break in a hundred pieces upon the cobblestones.

"With glee he stamped upon the fragments until they were but dust. Tears of gratitude filled my eyes. I knew I was the luckiest man in Babylon. Work, thou seest by this, in the time of my greatest distress, did prove to be my best friend. My willingness to work enabled me to escape from being sold to join the slave gangs upon the walls. It also so impressed thy grandfather, he selected me for his partner."

Then Hadan Gula questioned, "Was work my grandfather's secret key to the golden shekels?"

"It was the only key he had when I first knew him," Sharru Nada replied. "Thy grandfather enjoyed working. The gods appreciated his efforts and rewarded him liberally."

"I begin to see," Hadan Gula was speaking thoughtfully. "Work attracted his many friends, who admired his industry and the success it brought. Work brought him the honors he enjoyed so much in Damascus. Work brought him all those things I have approved. And I thought work was fit only for slaves."

"Life is rich, with many pleasures for men to enjoy," Sharru Nada commented. "Each has its place. I am glad that work is not reserved for slaves. Were that the case, I would be deprived of my greatest pleasure. Many things do I enjoy, but nothing takes the place of work."

Sharru Nada and Hadan Gula rode in the shadows of the towering walls up to the massive bronze gates of Babylon. At their approach, the gate guards jumped to attention and respectfully saluted an honored citizen. With head held high, Sharru Nada led the long caravan through the gates and up the streets of the city.

"I have always hoped to be a man like my grandfather," Hadan Gula confided to him. "Never before did I realize just what kind of man he was. This thou hast shown me. Now that I understand, I do admire him all the more and feel more determined to be like him. I fear I can never repay thee for giving me the true key to his success. From this day forth, I shall use his key. I shall start humbly as he started, which befits my true station far better than jewels and fine robes."

So saying, Hadan Gula pulled the jeweled baubles from his ears and the rings from his fingers. Then reining his horse, he dropped back and rode with deep respect behind the leader of the caravan.

---

# ❧ Dan ☙

This story might have been a little uncomfortable for some to hear. Tales of slavery, beatings, and abuse are hardly easy listening. It seems kind of a contrast to have a chapter about slavery called "The Luckiest Man in Babylon." Nonetheless, there are some core lessons here that can help us in our quest to become the richest man in Babylon.

The story starts with an old man, Sharru Nada, riding along with the young grandson of his former partner. The first part of the story shows the cultural differences between the older man and the younger man. The older man is looking at the young man and thinking, "Look at him. He's wearing jewelry like a woman, and he doesn't know a thing about hard work."

Meanwhile, the younger man is looking at the older man and thinking, "The poor guy. He thinks he has to work hard all the time. Doesn't he know that working is for slaves?" Clearly this kind of generation gap is present in every society. We still hear grandfathers telling their grandkids, "When I was a boy . . ." Some things never change.

How about you? Do you respect the wisdom of the generations before you, or do you believe that modern life has made the old values obsolete? Well, if you've learned anything from this program, you'll agree that strong values never go out of style.

The story goes on with Sharru Nada sharing the most important key to his success. It's two words: *hard work*. This chapter is intended to show the value that an industrious attitude can make on becoming the so-called luckiest man in Babylon.

In our generation, we have a wise man who's not so old, but he's definitely learned the secrets of success throughout hard work. It's Brian Tracy, and he's created an audio program called "The Twenty-One Success Secrets of Self-Made Millionaires." These are the common principles and practices of all men and women who become millionaires in one generation, and you're going to recognize them from the things we've learned in this program. Here are the twenty-one Success Secrets of Self-Made Millionaires, according to Brian Tracy.

1. Dream big dreams.
2. Develop a clear sense of direction.
3. See yourself as self-employed.
4. Do what you love to do.
5. Commit to excellence.
6. Work longer and harder.
7. Dedicate yourself to lifelong learning.
8. Pay yourself first.
9. Learn every detail of the business.
10. Dedicate yourself to serving others.
11. Be absolutely honest with yourself and others.
12. Set priorities and concentrate single-mindedly.
13. Develop a reputation for speed and dependability.
14. Be prepared to climb from peak to peak.
15. Practice self-discipline in all things.
16. Unlock your inborn creativity.
17. Get around the right people.
18. Take excellent care of your physical health.
19. Be decisive and action-oriented.
20. Never allow failure to be an option.
21. Pass the persistence test.

**Babylon Builder**

Now it's time for you to do an exercise. Do you love your work? Do you consider it to be one of your greatest pleasures? Sure, you may not be in your dream job, but what is your attitude about your work?

Now go get your journal and write down your honest thoughts about your attitude toward work.

No matter what you wrote in our journal, there is bound to be some room for improvement. Before you put your journal away, take a few minutes now to brainstorm ways that you can improve at your job. If a slave from Babylon can have an entrepreneurial attitude about baking, surely there are things you can do to improve your work performance.

What can you do, starting tomorrow, that will move your level of performance to excellent? Write it down now.

In all honesty, your attitude about work is an important indicator of whether or not you have the soul of a slave or the soul of a free man or woman. If you take your work seriously and do it with pride, no matter how menial the task, you will rise and succeed.

As we've mentioned in an earlier chapter, older people are having to return to the workforce in record numbers. In their generation, people had a different attitude about work than many do now. This is readily seen today.

What are some of the attitudes that may be different between the older generation and the younger generation? More importantly, how can you use these attitudes to stand out from the crowd? Here are just a few.

1. *Get to work on time.* Older workers were expected to show up on time for work every single day. Being late because of a personal problem or just not getting up on time was no excuse. If you want to excel at your job, get there early or on time every day, no exceptions.

2. *Put in a full day's work.* Today with the Internet, text messaging, and other technology, it's very easy for workers to waste hours each day on activities that aren't related to work. It's not OK to be texting your friends while at work, playing video games on your phone, or planning your next vacation. Put in a full day's work when you're at work, and your productivity will soar.

3. *Be open to feedback.* Instead of getting defensive or angry when someone gives you a suggestion for improvement, be open to it. Sure, the person giving you the feedback may be a jerk, but that doesn't mean that there isn't any truth to it. Get your ego out of the way, and tell the person, "Thanks for the feedback. I'll consider it." Then *do* consider it.

4. *Do the best you can in your current job.* Sure, you want a promotion. You probably deserve a raise and more responsibility, but you have to focus on being excellent at the job you're doing now instead of focusing on the next position.

Or, as Sharru Nada put it, "Life is rich, with many pleasures for men to enjoy. Each has its place. I am glad that work is not reserved for slaves. Were that the case, I would be deprived of my greatest pleasure. Many things do I enjoy, but nothing takes the place of work."

**Babylon Builder**

We've learned all about the value of hard work. The story was about slaves, but in some sense, we're all slaves. We're slaves to our bosses, slaves to our customers. It's not whom you work for or what you do for a living that matters. It's your attitude.

We learned the Twenty-One Success Secrets of Self-Made Millionaires from Brian Tracy. For your action steps, you took a good, hard look at your attitude about work, and you brainstormed some ideas to improve your work performance. You learned some action steps that you can take at work that incorporate the values of older workers into the modern workplace.

Let's recap now what we've learned. It's really amazing to think that the timeless lessons of wealth and abundance have been around for more than 8,000 years. Regardless of whether you're earning shekels or dollars or yen, the principles of finance and wealth are the same, just as was the case in Babylon.

Today we've forgotten the lessons taught in this program. Too many of us in modern society are concerned with short-term desires, the appearance of wealth instead of real wealth, trying to make a quick buck instead of building a legacy, and not caring about the quality of our work or the integrity of our relationships. We leave our dreams incomplete, like an unfinished chariot in the garage. Many of us have gotten completely off track, are buried under mounds of debt, and are depressed at the prospects for the future.

Luckily, though, we don't have to wait for our society to crumble to the ground. We have the power to turn it around on both a personal and a societal level.

By learning the secrets you've learned here, implementing them, and teaching them to others, you'll experience greater happiness and prosperity than ever before. It's not too late for you and for the rest of us, but it's going to take some tough thinking and some tough actions. Once you do them, you'll have the lasting kind of prosperity that is built on solid values and integrity.

It's about hard work, paying your debts, and taking care of yourself and your loved ones. If everyone in our culture did this, what kind of world would we have?

The folks in Babylon didn't have the advantages we do. In order to gain wisdom, they had to go seek out an expert. In the modern age, we don't need to go to a great hall of learning to gain the wisdom of our masters. It is available to us at a moment's notice, twenty-four hours a day, with a touch of a button or a click of a mouse. You can listen to a lecture or an audio podcast within five minutes of deciding to do so. Modern technology makes it easy to implement the lessons you've learned here.

As you're moving forward and you're implementing the lessons and techniques you've learned here, I encourage you to keep learning. Do as the other masters have done. Become a lifelong student. Listen to audio programs, podcasts, lectures, and shows. Examine our website at www.nightingale.com. Design your own personal development learning curriculum. Watch and support public television. Rent documentaries. Take teleclasses and in-person classes. Never stop learning, and never stop bettering yourself.

Your future is stretching ahead of you like an open road. Along the road are ambitions you wish to accomplish and desires you wish to gratify. To bring your ambitions and desires to fulfillment, you must be successful with money. If you use the principles you learned in this book, you'll leave your lean purse behind and enjoy a happier, wealthier life.

May the Goddess of Good Luck be with you always.

# About the Authors

**George Samuel Clason** was born in Louisiana, Missouri, in 1874. He attended the University of Nebraska and served in the United States Army during the Spanish-American War. Beginning a long career in publishing, he founded the Clason Map Company of Denver, Colorado, and published the first road atlas of the United States and Canada. In 1926, he issued the first of a famous series of pamphlets on thrift and financial success, using parables set in ancient Babylon to make each of his points. These were distributed in large quantities by banks and insurance companies and became familiar to millions. The most famous is "The Richest Man in Babylon," the parable from which the present volume takes its title. These "Babylonian parables" have become a modern inspirational classic. George S. Clason died in 1957.

**Dan Strutzel** is President of Inspire Productions, former Executive VP of Publishing at Nightingale-Conant Corporation, and a 25-year veteran of the personal development industry. Dan has worked closely with Bestselling personal development authors and speakers, including Tony Robbins, Brian Tracy, Jim Rohn, Robert Kiyosaki, Wayne Dyer and Zig Ziglar. Dan has a B.A. in English and Psychology from The University of Notre Dame.

Printed in the USA
CPSIA information can be obtained
at www.ICGtesting.com
JSHW012027140824
68134JS00033B/2920